GOSPEL REMIX

REACHING THE HIP HOP GENERATION

RALPH C. WATKINS

with Jason A. Barr Jr., Jamal-Harrison Bryant, William H. Curtis, Otis Moss III

THE GOSPEL REMIX
REACHING THE HIP HOP GENERATION

Library of Congress Cataloging-in-Publication Data
Watkins, Ralph C.
The Gospel remix : reaching the hip hop generation / Ralph C. Watkins, with Jason A. Barr, Jr.…[et al.].—1st ed.
p. cm.
Introduction—Section one: Walk this way: what is hip hop?—U don't know me: who is the hip hop generation?—My baby's momma: hip hop 2, the babies of the hip hop generation—A charge to keep I have: institutional barriers to reaching the hip hop generation—Bring 'em out: pastoring and evangelizing the hip hop generation—Section two: The hip hop pastor —Real big: the pastor as postmodern prophet—Words of wisdom : the pastor as father—Holla if you hear me: the pastor as peer—Bad boy for life from Puffy to Diddy: the pastor as model professional. Includes bibliographical references.
ISBN-13 978-0-8170-1507-7 (pbk.: alk. paper) 1. Church work with African Americans. 2. Hip-hop. 3. Christianity and culture. 4. Evangelistic work. I. Barr, Jason A. II. Title.
BV4468.2.A34W38 2006 259.089'96073—dc22
2006032658

Printed in the U.S.A. on recycled paper.
Second Printing, 2008.

ENDORSEMENTS

"*Theologically, I love the main points and the exegetical conclusions. Having a Bible-based resource for this topic is truly helpful!*"

—Christopher B. Brooks,
national coordinator, URBNET

"*...Provides introspective and diversified accounts of successful tools used by religious scholars and prominent black Evangelical pastors who have welcomed hip hop into their congregations....An insightful read that will open doors for more conversation on hip hop and interfaith dialogue.*"

—*Black Issues Book Review*

"*Ralph Watkins takes a revelatory look*...The Gospel Remix *defines hip hop and helps the reader understand how to reach out in authenticity.*"

—*Precious Times*

DEDICATIONS

This work is dedicated to the memory of Presiding Elder Arthur L. Maura, who always believed in me, and to my wife, Vanessa, and our children, Nastasia, Nicole, and Ralph III, for their love and support of the ministry God assigned our family.

—Ralph C. Watkins

This work is dedicated to the memory of my father, Rev. Jason A. Barr Sr., and my mother, Anne Reese Barr; and in appreciation of my wife and son, Kimberly Waddell Barr and Jason Barr III.

—Jason A. Barr Jr.

This work is dedicated to my queenly wife, Gizelle, for helping me to reign, and to my four princesses, Topaz, Grace, Angel, and Adore, who allow me to think that I rule!

—Jamal-Harrison Bryant

This offering is dedicated to my family, who provides inspiration and joy to my life; my pastor, Bishop Walter Thomas, for sharing his leadership with me; and to Mount Ararat Baptist Church, for ten years of support and for helping me become the leader God wants me to be.

—William H. Curtis

This work is dedicated to my wife and best friend, Monica Moss, my son, Elijah, and my daughter, Makayla, who demonstrate the power and joy of love, prayer, and friendship every day the sun rises and sets in my life.

—Otis Moss III

CONTENTS

introduction
THROUGH THE EYES OF A DJ: PEEKING IN ON HIP HOP CULTURE

Then drew near unto him all the publicans and sinners for to hear him. And the Pharisees and scribes murmured, saying, "This man receiveth sinners, and eateth with them."

—Luke 15:1-2 KJV

I am drawn to start this work out of this biblical text. This text has always intrigued me; I have always wanted to know why sinners were drawn to Jesus. Why did they fight to draw near to hear him? The easy answer is, after all, he was Jesus. The more difficult assignment is to turn the mirror on ourselves and the present-day church and pose a series of questions. We know he was Jesus, but the question remains, What did he do that we can learn from? How can we, like him, attract folk to hear the gospel? Why does it appear that so many people are repelled by our message and ministry? We have the best deal in town. We have the only true Savior; we are his church; we are his body; shouldn't we attract sinners just like Jesus did? Didn't he give us his power and charisma?

The second thing that has always puzzled me about this text was the Pharisees' response. They criticized Jesus for his ability to attract sinners. They murmured and complained about his sitting and eating with sinners. Why weren't they excited and supportive of his reaching out and touching those who needed his teaching and healing touch? Why did they think they were better than those whom they classified as sinners? Do we have Pharisees and scribes in the church today? Do we have folk who complain about our desire to reach out and touch sinners? Would we be talked about if we hung out with sinners? Do we hang out with enough sinners to be talked about?

These are the very questions that have fueled my zeal to evangelize the hip hop generation. As a college professor and later a seminary professor, I was teaching about hip hop in the academy and making appeals to churches about reaching the hip hop generation. In my classes and workshops, I was continually looking in the mirror and asking myself, How can I get closer to the hip hop generation? As much as I studied their music and culture, I, as a man in his early forties, still felt removed. How could I sit with them as Jesus sat with tax collectors and sinners? How could I bond with them and begin to empathize with their lot in life? How did I move from the objective, passionate study of a culture and a people to being in fellowship with them?

Then I listened to KRS One, who said in the video *Rhyme and Reason,* "Rap is something you do, but hip hop is something you live."[1] That really convicted me. How can I live hip hop and still be a Christian? Not only be a Christian, but here I am a preacher: How can I live or be hip hop and be a preacher? How can I get any closer than I am? As a sociologist who taught a course on hip hop, I was already feeling guilty for simply listening to the music. I had reasoned that I had to listen to it to study it and relate to the hip hop generation. Now I was being pushed to be more like Jesus and sit with the hip hop generation. I had to be with them authentically in love so that I could reach out to them in Christ.

The question became *How?* It was here that my training as a sociologist and a preacher began to come together. As a sociologist, I have always admired the work of Kenneth Clark, who gave us the term "involved participant observer."[2] In sociology, we talk a lot about being a participant observer in our research. Participant observation is a research method in which researchers take part in the social phenomenon being studied but maintain their objectivity and distance. Clark said the involved participant observer goes a step further. Involved participant observers are not there simply to observe as distant objective researchers, but they become a part of the community and have a vested interest in its future. They are not removed, detached scholars sitting in to gaze at humans as subjects, but rather they work to be members of that community. Their feelings, their wishes, and their desires move them to become active agents in that community as they work to guide, direct, and shape the very community they are studying.

How do I become an involved participant observer in the hip hop community? How do I take part in hip hop? How do I get in, to sit in, to be involved? It was here that my love for music in general and my love for some of the music of the hip hop generation began to provide an answer. I confessed my love for this music and the culture and then began to ask God, How can I use this to make a difference for you and the kingdom? I prayed and asked God to show me a way, a vehicle that could transport me to the world of the hip hop generation. I wanted to be able to get as close to them as I could. I wanted to sit with them and eat with them. I wanted to enter their world to learn how to love them as Christ would. I wanted to learn their language and culture so that I could better understand them. I believed that if I could better understand them, I could find ways by the power of the Holy Spirit to reach them. During this period, I meditated and prayed over two passages of Scripture, 1 Corinthians 9:19-23 and Matthew 9:9-13.

> For though I am free from all men, *I have made myself a servant to all, that I might win the more;* and to the Jews I became as a Jew, that I might win Jews; to those who are under the law, as under the law, that I might win those who are under the law; to those who are without law, as without law (not being without law toward God, but under law toward Christ), that I might win those who are without law; to the weak I became as weak, that I might win the weak. I have become all things to all men, that I might by all means save some. Now this I do for the gospel's sake, that I may be partaker of it with you. (1 Corinthians 9:19-23 NKJV, emphasis added)

In this first passage, I was struck by Paul's insistence on being a servant to all. How am I or how are we to be a servant to the hip hop generation? How do we reach them? How do we become them? Paul became what he witnessed to. He became a Jew, a Greek, as one who was weak to win people to Christ. The revelation to me was that I had to find a way to become hip hop to reach those who are hip hop, while maintaining my faith and witness. But how?

Then, as I moved on to the second passage, I was once again struck by Jesus' walking and calling sinners to follow him. Jesus didn't turn them away but instead welcomed them and attracted them. The fact that Jesus took time to sit with them stood out, and even more compelling was that he sat with them in their homes, in their own environment. He went to them, sat with them, and ate with them at their tables. He didn't invite them to the church or his location; he went to their location.

> As Jesus passed on from there, He saw a man named Matthew sitting at the tax office. And He said to him, "Follow Me." So he arose and followed Him.
>
> Now it happened, as Jesus sat at the table in the house, that behold, many tax collectors and sinners came and sat down with Him and His disciples. And when the Pharisees saw it, they said to His disciples, "Why does your Teacher eat with tax collectors and sinners?"
>
> When Jesus heard that, He said to them, "Those who are well have no need of a physician, but those who are sick. But go and learn what this means: 'I desire mercy and not sacrifice.' For I did not come to call the righteous, but sinners, to repentance." (Matthew 9:9-13 NKJV)

How do I sit at the table with people from the hip hop generation? They need help, and I need help. When I look at hip hop culture and what it is producing, I see the illnesses as well as the health. I see the sickness that needs to be healed. We need to go and sit with them, touch them, love them, and heal them. They are in need of a doctor. These comments are not meant to degrade or put down the culture but are an honest assessment. There is much good in the hip hop culture, but there are also parts of it that are unhealthy and not good for our youth or our community. As much as we must celebrate hip hop, we mustn't look at it or any other cultural production uncritically. We must bring the values and principles of the Bible to bear on our interrogation of cultural phenomena. The question for me, as I looked at the good and bad of the culture, was, How do I gain access?

To sit at the table with sinners brings critique, skepticism, and misunderstanding. This is the case because in the culture of the church we have erected walls between the worldly and the spiritual. We are called out of the world, and so we try to keep the world out of the church. Most churches fellowship with other churches, not with the unsaved and the unchurched. We are taught to welcome folk to church, to bring people to church, but we aren't fully equipped to take Christ to the world. As I was laboring in prayer over this call, I knew I was putting myself in the line of fire for intense ridicule. How can a preacher be ______? Just fill in the blank.

When God came to me, it was clear. The seat to sit with them as an involved participant observer was through my teaching, preaching, and DJing. I had to live these two passages, 1 Corinthians 9:19-23 and Matthew 9:9-13. I had to become hip hop by embracing one of the pillars of the culture. The vehicle to reach people was through the music, so I had to become a DJ. The first problem was that I was not a DJ. So I had another project: I had to become a DJ. I began to do my research on DJing. I read books, and then I began to purchase equipment. The first dance I did was at an elementary school; then I progressed to a high school, then to a local club, and finally to doing dances at the local college.

The move was on, but I was still very uncomfortable. What type of music do I play? Do I play the edited versions (no cursing, clean cuts), or do I play the unedited versions? What was my motive?

What was I trying to learn? What was I trying to promote? Do I preach as I DJ? Do I simply play what is requested and sit back as a sociologist, study what I see, and report back? Do I get involved in the moment? Do I become the music? What is this music doing to me? What does it do to me to be a preacher being exposed to so much sin? What does this say about my witness? Is this a place for a preacher? These and so many questions had to be dealt with continually in prayer and study. In all honesty, I still struggle with these questions as I explore this ministry.

Through prayer and study, my dilemma was resolved for the moment. I separated my work and call into two connected compartments. The first compartment was to be continual, always evolving, and would also feed back into the second compartment. The first compartment required me to enter the culture as a sociologist who is a Christian. I would take my faith with me, but as a sociologist who is an involved participant observer. I would enter the club or the party as a DJ. I would play what was requested. To play edited or unedited versions of the music was to be determined by the age appropriateness of the crowd. I was entering the culture initially not to change it but rather to engage it and study it. I was there as a student first, as an involved participant observer. I would become hip hop by playing and listening to the music. This would put me in an initial position to begin to understand the hip hop generation. I had to seek to understand them if I was to learn to love them from where they were—not from where I wanted them to be.

I was to enter the venue as a DJ. I bought music as a DJ. I became a member of the American Academy of DJs. I started my own DJ business. I went in and dressed similar to hip hoppers. I studied their music, listened to and charted the songs they requested. I felt the music as I played it. I got into each set and learned how to keep the party *crunk,* or jumping.

A turning point came on March 26, 2005, Saturday night, the night before Easter. I found myself hosting my biggest and most successful party to date. My daughter and her teenage high school club, Delta Alpha Zeta (DAZ), asked me to host their Spring Jump Off Dance. I agreed. We secured the hall at the university, with cosponsorship of the Sociology Club. Delta Alpha Zeta handled the advertising, and the place was packed. Here I was in the biggest venue I had been to date, and the test was, What had I learned? Could I be hip hop, have a good set, keep the party *crunk*, learn while being in the moment, and then take what I had learned and allow it to inform ministry and evangelism?

Let me back up and clarify: Prior to my conversion, as a young man, I didn't frequent clubs or parties. I was content to sit with my friends, get high, and listen to music. The club or party scene was never my thing. I was always uncomfortable in club environments. I was never one to dance, but here I found myself in the very place I never thought I would be. I am reminded every time I go to DJ that I was called to study this scene and become a part of it so that we can win souls for Christ.

Prior to my big March 26, 2005, event, I learned that playlists are crucial to every party. You have to have a list of the right music to play for that crowd. For this event, I had consulted several sources, as I did with every event, to help me develop a good playlist. We had a great playlist. Because the crowd was going to be older teenagers and college students, I decided to play some edited and unedited versions of the music. The party built slowly. I took my time to work the party up. I sat back and watched the floor fill. The girls were out dancing, but the guys were lurking outside the party. The party started at 8:00 p.m., and it was scheduled to go until 1:30 a.m. Around 9:30 p.m., the small crowd began to form. We started playing some booty-shaking music. We played cuts that girls would dance to. The girls attract the boys to the dance floor and into the party.

Around 10:30 p.m., the crowd began to swell. We had a critical mass on the inside and the outside. I now had the challenge of picking the right mix of music to keep my inside crowd on the floor while attracting those outside inside, and keeping the party moving. It was time to turn it up. A mix of *crunk* music, club bangers, and dance music was now the order of the night. My wife and I sat back on the stage, and we began to work together to build the right mix of music. We watched who came on the floor and who left. We watched as the fever pitch began to swell. With each song, more people joined the floor. When I would cue up the next song and cut it in, you would see hands go up, people shout and begin to move. The party goers knew these songs. They knew them word for word. They rapped and sang with the artist as the song played. I had them. They were dancing and having a good time. I watched like a student while playing music like a DJ.

As the night progressed, the party was packed. At midnight, I was getting very few requests; about five requests had come all night. I was hitting on all cylinders. I was on the inside. The lack of requests and the response to the music meant that I had them: I knew what to play, when to play, how to mix it and keep the party going. DJing is as much an art as it is a science. You have to feel the party, know the crowd, know the music, and be in the moment to build the party. As we moved into Easter morning, ironically enough I put on a song by the artist T. I. entitled "Bring 'Em Out."[3] The dance floor swelled to capacity, and then before I knew it, a young man was swung on; a fight had broken out on the dance floor.

The young man came tumbling toward the stage where I was playing the music. The video projector was knocked to the side. My wife shouted, "Ralph, it's a fight." I stopped the music and jumped down from the stage. I forced my way between the warring camps, pushing the aggressor back and yelling expletives. As I pushed him back, I made my way to the back of the room and cut on the lights. I then ran back to the stage, got the wireless microphone, called for the police. The police arrived, and people told them that there had been gunshots and that they saw a gun. Therefore, the police came in yelling to shut down the party. I immediately yelled back at the police, "You don't have that power; you haven't talked to me." An officer informed me of the report of gunshots. I corrected the misinformation. There were no gunshots, and there was no gun. I am always a bit defensive of this generation. The police came in with their preconceived notions that I had to correct and challenge. This was no big fight. It was simply a misunderstanding between two individuals. I had previously yelled out on the microphone that all those who were fighting were going to jail and those who wanted to stay and party were welcome.

After my adrenaline began to subside and I saw many partiers leaving, I decided to agree with the police and call it all off. I said to the crowd, "Since a few of our brothers and sisters don't know how to act, we have to call it a night." I wished them happy Easter and began to work with the police to clear the room and the parking lot. I had found in working with parties that the later you go, the more trouble you are bound to have. I have also found that when you begin to clear the party, you have to work just as hard to clear the parking lot. The parking lot is a volatile place where encounters and arguments that started inside are taken outside. It took us at least an hour to clear the place out and get our gear packed up. We left the spot around 1:30 a.m. to get a few hours of sleep before going to early morning Easter service.

When we got home, we talked, laughed, and processed the dance. My kids commented on my DJing. My older daughter, who had come home from college with her boyfriend for Easter, said, "Daddy, that's the best DJing we ever had at a DAZ party." I felt affirmed by my kids. At the first party I did for their group, my younger daughter was ridiculed by my ineffectiveness as a DJ. This time my growth was obvious, as I had read and listened to hip hoppers at every event to learn what it was they wanted to hear. I played what they wanted to hear even if I didn't want to hear it. After a morning of reflection, we went off to bed around 2:30 a.m. We arose early Sunday morning to be at church for 7:45 a.m. worship.

During the worship service, we celebrated the resurrection of Christ, and the preacher in me started to come out as I reflected on last night and the connection with this morning. "If I be lifted up, I will draw all men unto me." This is what the church was to do. We were to lift Christ up. How do we lift Christ up to the crowd I was with last night? How do we reach them? How do we save them? How do we draw them to church as I had drawn them to that party and to that dance floor? I had sat with them. Now what do I do with what I had learned while at the table? How do I engage the second compartment of my work and call?

The second compartment of this work was to move from the table where I had sat and learned and progress to take what I had learned and use it to evangelize the hip hop generation.

As I sat in worship thinking about the death and resurrection of Jesus Christ, I couldn't forget all that had happened the previous night. It wasn't all good. Someone could have been seriously injured. That someone could have been me or any member of my family. I remembered that as I rode away from the dance last night, my wife and I celebrated that no one had been seriously injured. But we then quickly remarked, "But someone died at a club or party somewhere tonight." Someone dies in the club every weekend. This is why our work is so important: we have to go into the club to get them out of the club. We have to invade the club culture if we are going to reclaim them for Christ. How do we do this?

We reclaim the lost by sitting with them, loving them, learning about them, and then sharing the gospel with them. I had to take what I was learning from the inside and teach it to others. I had to find successful pastoral models, church and parachurch models that were reaching the hip hop generation. I had to develop a theology of hip hop so we could talk with the hip hop generation and teach them about God in a way they understand and that moves them toward the truth. I had to discover and design ways for those who care about the hip hop generation to find means to effectively evangelize them. I was convinced that I couldn't do this if I didn't fully understand the culture in its rawest form. Then I had to work with the hip hop generation to develop a plan to reach their peers. This was part two of our work. The first and second parts must be held in creative and divine tension.

Tolerating some of the music and parts of the culture is very difficult for me. There are times when I am playing a song and it is so vulgar that I cringe at every other word. I look out on the dance floor and see people become what I am playing, and I immediately judge myself, the music, and the dancers. I have to fight this urge and suspend such judgment because I have been given the privilege to peek in on hip hop culture. God has allowed me to see it, so that I can report what I have found and then work with the church to reach the hip hop generation. I have to bear the critique and misunderstanding of hundreds to save thousands. I heard this call clearly. I don't want to give up my weekends, play ungodly music, put me and my family in harm's way—but I believe that is my call.

The preacher who was a DJ was born again and sent to a new mission field. I was called to go to the clubs and back to the church. This change meant it was not unusual for me to do a workshop at a church on Saturday, do a dance/party Saturday night, and then preach on Sunday morning. This metaphoric circle of being in the world but not of the world came to inform my work and subsequently this book. I was to use what I learned for Christ and his church. I had to know the world to reach the world. I had to go to the nation of hip hop and become an honorary citizen to be able to extend an invitation to them to become a member of the kingdom.

In this book, the contributors and I share our stories and what we have learned as a testimony. Like the apostle John, I can only testify to what I have seen and learned (1 John 4:12-16). I share my testimony with the body of Christ in hopes that it will equip us to reach a generation that we are losing. The hip hop generation is finding the church increasingly irrelevant, and I will argue that they are developing a religious and spiritual life outside of the church. We *can* reach them, and we *can* save them. The intent of this book, first of all, is to help us understand the hip hop generation. Second, we will share models that have worked in reaching them. We pray that what you read will inform your vision, hope, and divine creativity as we seek and save that which is lost. We are called to love, and this book is ultimately a call to love (1 John 4:7-21).

> And Jesus came and spoke to them, saying, "All authority has been given to Me in heaven and on earth. Go therefore and make disciples of all the nations, baptizing them in the name of the Father and of the Son and of the Holy Spirit, teaching them to observe all things that I have commanded you; and lo, I am with you always, even to the end of the age." (Matthew 28:18-20 NKJV)

> Amen.

NOTES

1. Peter Spirer, *Rhyme and Reason,* DVD (Miramax Entertainment, 2000).
2. Kenneth Clark, *Dark Ghetto: Dilemmas of Social Power* (New York: Harper, 1965), xvi–xxv.
3. T. I., "Bring 'Em Out," *Urban Legend,* CD (Atlantic Records, 2005).

CHAPTER 1
WALK THIS WAY: WHAT IS HIP HOP?

Therefore, I urge you, brothers, in view of God's mercy, to offer your bodies as living sacrifices, holy and pleasing to God—this is your spiritual worship. Do not conform any longer to the pattern of this world, but be transformed by the renewing of your mind. Then you will be able to test and approve what God's will is—his good, pleasing and perfect will.

—Romans 12:1-2 NIV

As we start our journey together, the text that greets us is Romans 12:1-2. This text speaks to what I have found to be one of our deepest issues with hip hop and the hip hop generation. How do we deal with the patterns of the world—namely, the hip hop world—while not conforming to it? The tension of reaching out to the hip hop generation and dealing with hip hop in a biblical and faithful way is the centerpiece of this book. We want to help the church pray through how God will use it to reach the hip hop generation as God renews the church. To faithfully engage in this quest, we must be willing to be renewed in our minds and spirits as we take a fresh look at hip hop and the hip hop generation. Taking this new look will call on us to offer God our spiritual service or worship as we submit to what God is saying to us as God directs us in this next major move in the life of the African American church. We are challenged to be transformed by God as God renews us and shows us how to be faithful while simultaneously reaching hip hoppers.

The questions I hear most as I go out and speak about the African American church and the hip hop generation are, How do we deal with the culture outside the church? Do we bring it in the church?

Do we accept hip hop hook, line, and sinker? Do we critique hip hop? What do we do with the sexism, cursing, and misogyny in hip hop? How can we embrace and use something that makes us look so bad? All of these are legitimate questions, and we will deal with them up front.

The church has to struggle continually with the appropriation of culture and the integrity of God's church. This has always been our struggle, and in this book we invite every congregation and pastor to enter that struggle as God leads them. The African American church has dealt with similar issues in the past. We had to deal with Thomas Dorsey and his leadership in the development of gospel music. It was Dr. Dorsey who took the feel of the blues and applied it to church music. The African American church faced this struggle with the advent of James Cleveland and Edwin Hawkins as the church had to deal with the next wave of gospel music. There was a great uproar around the song "Oh Happy Day." Then came Kirk Franklin, and yet another struggle emerged. Struggle over the infusion of new music styles and popular culture is nothing new to the African American church.

In each phase of this evolution, from Thomas Dorsey to Kirk Franklin, the African American church has remained faithful, but we haven't shied away from asking God to help us deal with these difficult issues. What we have found is that at each phase of musical development, the church has remained true to the gospel while learning how to embrace the culture in ways that are biblical as well as protecting the integrity of God's church. We believe that once again the church will rise to the occasion. The church should not accept any popular cultural manifestations hook, line, and sinker. We are to be appreciative and critical simultaneously. Therefore the church has the responsibility, as given us by God, to engage the culture in such a way that we can look at what it has to offer and then ask questions that lead us to find out how God wants to use what is outside to bless the inside.

The church has to critique and deal with hip hop. We have to stand as a corrective to the ills of the culture. As we move to critique and correct, we may want to think about what Michael Eric Dyson calls us to in his book on Tupac: a practice of "ethical patience." According to Dyson, "ethical patience is the ability to hear and understand popular culture on its own terms before seeking to critique it."[1] We have to seek to understand what people are saying through the culture before we critique the culture. In essence, we engage in a two-part exercise. The first is a listening exercise in which we try to understand what the hip hop generation is saying about itself; we seek first to understand the depth and breadth of hip hop. We also seek to see the beauty, pain, truthfulness, meaningfulness, goodness, and justice in the message of hip hop. Only after we have heard their story—while fighting to hold back our critique, as difficult as this is—can we then move to a more complete engagement with the art as we critique what we have heard.

A major struggle I have found with hip hop and the church has been dealing with the overt sexism, misogyny, and negative presentation of African Americans in the music. This is an area of justified concern, one that we must address. Recording companies and artists who produce negative images of our people must be held accountable. As we hold them accountable, we must also contextualize their work in the larger culture as well as situating them historically. The negative and oversexualized images we see in hip hop are a part of a trend in a popular culture that is becoming progressively more vulgar and visual. Should we single out hip hop while not engaging the larger culture that is producing hypersexual images of young people? Is it the church's responsibility also to engage the larger culture that calls for and produces such images? We may want to think about what these images say about our people and how we can appropriately engage the hip hop generation in dialogue about these images. How can we get the hip hop generation to hear us? What is the value in our hearing them fully before we seek to be heard? Will our critique be heard or justified if we haven't at least made an attempt to engage both hip hop culture and the larger context of popular culture?

As African Americans, we also have to be honest about the difficulty we have in dealing with sexuality and sexual images of ourselves. This book is not the place to deal with this issue, but our inability or lack of willingness to tackle the issues surrounding the portrayal of the black body and black women is central to our being able to deal with hip hop. To those who want to think more deeply about these issues, I recommend two books: Kelley Brown Douglas's *Sexuality and the Black Church* and Patricia Hill Collins's *Black Sexual Politics*.[2] Suffice it to say at this point that part of the problem we may have with the sexual images in hip hop videos is linked to the African American community's own hang-ups about sex, sexuality, and sexual images, past and present, presented of us. Churches may want to have conversations about sexuality in the African American community as a way of getting at this issue. We might also want to talk about how the hip hop generation is defining its sexuality as it is presented in its music, movies, and videos. Do they see their sexuality and love relationships differently than did their elders, and can we make room in the church to discuss these questions?

As I have talked with church leaders about hip hop another issue that has been raised is the language that the rappers use. How do we deal with the cursing in the music and the negative references to African American women? This is a serious issue, and there are at least two ways to look at it. One way to look at this is by asking how they use these words. What do these words mean to them? How are they making meaning with their word choices? Another way of looking at the use of foul language is to call it a sin, rebuke them, and correct them for such use of the language. I am sure there are many options in between the two extremes, but the point that must not be missed is that the use of language is a way of making meaning in hip hop. We have to ask ourselves, How can we understand what they are trying to say if we don't listen to how they say it? This may mean that we buy edited versions of the music and guess what the curse words are, or it may mean that we buy the unedited versions and engage in Dyson's call for ethical patience. Regardless of which options we choose, I don't think we can choose not to listen, because if we choose not to listen, we choose not to know how they are making meaning in their world.

The complaints about hip hop, which are well founded, are typically linked to segments of the music and culture. The party rap or club bangers are the songs that get the most air time. These songs and videos are meant to make people dance, and they tend to be the most explicit. Those who see only this part of hip hop have to make a judgment about the art form and culture by sampling a small piece of hip hop culture. Hip hop is more diverse than what we see on music television or what is attacked in mass media. Hip hop is deeper and richer than what the casual observer may realize. For starters, there are at least eleven types or genres of rap music:

1. East Coast Rap
2. West Coast Rap
3. Dirty South Rap
4. Third Coast Rap/Houston
5. Political Rap
6. Jazz Rap
7. Bohemian Rap
8. *Reggaeton* Rap
9. Holy Hip Hop
10. Midwest Rap
11. Party/Booty Rap—what we see most and what fuels the most critique

Even with these eleven types of rap music, it is fair to say that the most popular forms are the ones we will tend to have the most trouble with. The concerns we have are legitimate and not to be trivialized. As we engage these more popular forms of rap music, we must at least try to suspend our judgment as we seek to develop a lexicon so that we can talk to those who enjoy the music. This means we have to fight to engage the culture without dismissing it, while acknowledging it is difficult to listen to and hard to understand.

The less popular genres—by which we mean they don't sell in high volumes or get the radio/television play that the more popular forms do—also need to be engaged. The more thoughtful or political forms of rap—called "conscious rap"—are touching the older members of the hip hop generation. We will talk more about the hip hop generations in chapters 2 and 3, but we must not forget that the older members of the hip hop generation are between the ages of thirty and forty-two. The more mature hip hoppers are not listening to booty music as much as they are listening to forms of conscious rap. They are still heavily influenced by the music and the culture, but in ways different from their younger hip hop siblings. To truly understand the hip hop generation, both the young and the more mature, we must come to grips with their culture. We have to move beyond the music and look to the broader hip hop culture.

When we move beyond the music and push for a richer definition of hip hop, what do we find? We find that hip hop is a culture. It involves morals, values, ideas, ideals, ideology, and a way of life. It is an African American youth cultural production that was birthed out of a sociopolitical context of the late 1970s. The sociopolitical-economic timing was important. Hip hop was born at the end of the civil rights period. The United States was in a reactionary political posture. The White House had just experienced disgrace at the criminal hands of President Richard M. Nixon and then moved into the time of presidents Gerald Ford and Jimmy Carter. After President Carter's term, the country made a hard, twelve-year turn to the right. The nation was led by President Ronald Reagan for eight years, and then his conservative understudy assumed the helm for four years. President George W. Bush, like President Reagan, was a true conservative. This conservative agenda forced hip hoppers to speak up. While the middle class, black and white, was running for the suburbs, hip hoppers were left in the inner cities with an economy that was going global. Industrial jobs were drying up, public education was being undermined, social services were being withdrawn, and Clarence

Thomas was the chief of the Equal Employment Opportunity Commission attacking affirmative action and civil rights.

New York is considered the birthplace of hip hop culture. A DJ from the ghettos of Jamaica, a son of dancehall music, saw that what was happening in New York repeated what he had witnessed in Jamaica. DJ Kool Herc, born Clive Campbell in 1954 in Kingston, Jamaica, grew up in the same Trenchtown ghetto as Bob Marley. The dancehall had been the place of release, fun, and parties for Jamaicans. DJ Kool Herc brought that same ethos to America when, in the late 1970s, he started throwing outdoor parties in the South Bronx. These parties were meant to bring people together to have fun and relieve the tedium of life for the poor. In his quest to extend the party and the dancing, DJ Kool Herc discovered the breakdown portion of the song. He began to mix two records to extend the breakdown portion; hence, we get break dancers dancing to the break beats.

After DJ Kool Herc came many who extended the culture. We can't go on without mentioning Afrika Bambaataa, who founded the Zulu Nation to bring the warring factions of New York City gangs together. The early hip hop culture was one of bringing people together to have fun and celebrate African Diasporic culture. There was Grand Master Flash, who perfected the peek-a-boo or cueing system. There was Grand Wizard Theodore, the student of Grand Master Flash, who invented the scratch. These way-makers were the foundation of hip hop culture, along with the graffiti artists, break dancers, and thousands of young people who embraced and grew the culture—the unnamed turntablists, rappers, dancers, and party supporters. Out of this process of indigenous cultural development came what we now call hip hop.

According to KRS One, the teacher of hip hop, hip hop culture is composed of nine elements:

> True Hiphop is a term that describes the independent collective consciousness of a specific group of inner-city people. Ever growing, it is commonly expressed through such elements as:

> [1]Breakin' (Breakdancing), [2]Emceein' (Rap), [3]Graffiti art (aerosol art), [4]Dejayin', [5]Beatboxin', [6]Street Fashion, [7]Street Language, [8]Street Knowledge, and [9]Street Entrepreneurialism. Hiphop is not just music and dance, nor is Hiphop a product to be bought and sold. Discovered by Kool DJ Herc in the Bronx, New York around 1972, and established as a community of peace, love, unity, and having fun by Afrika Bambaataa through the Zulu Nation in 1974, Hiphop is an independent and unique community, an empowering behavior, and an international culture.[3]

KRS One defines hip hop culture in its broadest and purest form. Hip hop is an international culture, though hip hop and its music are the most recent wave of development of African American popular music. Its roots are in the African Diaspora, the disaporic experience of African culture. The nine elements form the core of this culture. Around this core, hip hop culture continues to evolve as the second generation of rappers and hip hop leaders are now taking center stage. The old heads are being honored as they pass the mantle. As the stage is being filled by new artists, the core and the carriers of the culture remain the rappers or emcees. They are the carriers of the culture because it is the creative power of language that defines and sustains hip hop culture. Molefi Kete Asante has termed this power the *nommo*, which is the power inherent in words to create worlds.[4] Just as God stepped out and created the heavens and earth as he spoke creation into existence, rappers or emcees are designing and defining their world by the use of language.

The role and power of the emcee is summed up best by stic.man in *The Art of Emcee-ing:* "An emcee is a creator, innovator, communicator, orator, translator, teacher, visionary, representative, thinker, convincer, speaker, story teller, messenger, poet, griot, a writer, master of ceremonies, historian, leader, reporter, a vocal instrument, philosopher, fan, an observer, a student, therapist, social analyst, evangelist, a minister, a professor, sales person, motivator, mack, chalmer, host, and artist all in one!"[5]

The emcee or the rapper has the power of the word. The power of the word is central to the establishment, nurture, and continuation of the culture. The Kenyan scholar Ngugi wa Thiong'o says, "Language, any language, has a dual character: it is both a means of communication and a carrier of culture."[6] Therefore, if we hope to understand hip hop, we have to get into the language of hip hop. If we love our young people, we have to ask ourselves, Have we heard them? And how will we hear them? When we listen to what they are saying, we are beginning to understand their world. We are empowered to see as they see, hear as they hear, and see the world as they see it. When we listen to music, we understand how it is transmitting values.

Hip hop is a culture that informs the lives of those who consider themselves hip hop. When we watch how they live, we see the power in the culture. We see hip hop in the way young people dress. Hip hop is an oversized culture. It is big; therefore hip hoppers wear clothes that are too big. They wear their white tee shirts on the outside. They wear boots, but they don't go hiking. They experiment with new styles and trends on a monthly basis. Their recording artists have a typical shelf life of two to three compact discs. Watching music is the order of the day for them; my generation listened to music, but not this generation. Hip hop culture informs how they walk, how they drive, and how they boom their music in their car with the subwoofer in the back. The culture is pervasive.

One of my students, Pastor Jack Hakimian, is famous for saying that hip hop is a consciousness. It informs the way members of the hip hop generation see themselves. Hip hop informs their worldview and is a mindset, with both good and negative components. So as we look at the nine elements of hip hop culture, let's remember that these elements are expressed in a lifestyle, one that is thoroughly American. Many of the values we see in the larger American culture are only exaggerated in hip hop. Hip hop culture is not something we can ignore; it touches every aspect of the lives of the hip hop generation. They live hip hop. Some would say, "I *am* hip hop."

It is important that we listen in on the culture as we live out our love for those in our community under forty years of age. This culture, with the nine elements mentioned by KRS One, is a growing culture with mass appeal. Its tentacles are reaching around the globe in all communities as it blurs race, class, and ethnicity. It is a culture that has great value and even demonstrates some redemptive qualities. Now, who are these people that are taken by hip hop culture? What do they look like? What is their story? Their story is important because the truth of who they are lies in the story. A part of that story is in the art and culture of hip hop, and another part of that story is in their historical situation. In the next two chapters, we will talk about who the hip hop generation is, what they like and don't like, and what has shaped who they have become.

This is a love story. We can never lock eyes with any member of the hip hop generation whom God doesn't love. We are called by God to love; to say that we love without reaching out and embracing them and their culture calls into question the strength and reality of our love. Do we love them enough to seek to understand them? Will we love their language so that we will talk to them? Will we love them in the shape in which they come to us? How will we show them we love them?

> Beloved, let us love one another, for love is of God; and everyone who loves is born of God and knows God. He who does not love does not know God, for God is love. In this the love of God was manifested toward us, that God has sent His only begotten Son into the world, that we might live through Him. In this is love, not that we loved God, but that He loved us and sent His Son to be the propitiation for our sins. Beloved, if God so loved us, we also ought to love one another. (1 John 4:7-11 NKJV)
>
> Amen.

NOTES

1. Michael Eric Dyson, *Holler If You Hear Me: Searching for Tupac Shakur* (New York: Basic Civitas Books, 2002), 211.

2. Kelly Brown Douglas, *Sexuality and the Black Church: A Womanist Perspective* (Maryknoll, N.Y.: Orbis, 1999); Patricia Hill Collins, *Black Sexual Politics: African Americans, Gender, and the New Racism* (New York: Routledge, 2004).
3. KRS One, *Ruminations* (New York: Welcome Rain Publishers, 2003), 179–80.
4. Molefi Kete Asante, *The Afrocentric Idea* (Philadelphia: Temple University Press, 1998), 60.
5. stic.man, *The Art of Emcee-ing* (Atlanta: Boss Up Publishers, 2005), 13.
6. Ngugi wa Thiong'o, *Decolonising the Mind: The Politics of Language in African Literature* (Portsmouth, N.H.: Heinemann, 1986), 13.

CHAPTER 2
U DON'T KNOW ME: WHO IS THE HIP HOP GENERATION?

"This is My commandment, that you love one another as I have loved you."

—John 15:12 NKJV

As we look more closely at the hip hop generation, we now ask, Who are they? What defines the hip hop generation? What are their sociocultural markers? This chapter will give keys to understanding the hip hop generation. It also breaks down the characteristics that mark this generation as different from the former generation. Things they like and don't like are outlined. The things that excite them and attract them will be clearly defined in such a way that those definitions can inform the effective evangelization of the hip hop generation. We will accept Bakari Kitwana's definition of the hip hop generation as those born between 1965 and 1986.[1] When we look at Bakari's generational time frame for the hip hop generation, we realize we are not talking about teenagers but about young adults.

As we think about getting to know this group, we must first reignite our love for them. As I said in the first chapter, this is a love story, as we extend the love of God to those of the hip hop generation. As we look at them in love, our gaze should be toward the young adults who are absent from a significant number of mainline, older churches.

In my work with churches, I have found that many of my peers and those older than I are angry with the hip hop generation. Yet I have also found that they are willing to love through their anger. A root of this anger could be described as disappointment. The civil rights generation had high hopes for the hip hop generation. They wanted those following them to achieve on par with or above their own level of success. The civil rights generation fought to open doors and break down barriers to ensure the next generations' success. When the civil rights generation sees pants hanging down, hears speakers bumping in cars, and notices girls with thongs rising out of the back of their pants, they look in disgust. I don't want to dismiss these feelings. I only want to ask, What do we do with these feelings? These feelings are rooted in our love for young African Americans. We want to see them do better and be better. We love them, and now we must put that love in action as we get to know them a little better so that we can come to understand their behavior and better relate to them. I am not asking you to condone their dress or behavior, but I am asking you to read along with me and at least try to understand and appreciate who these young people really are.

HOW CLASS, RACE, AND AGE SHAPE THE HIP HOP IDENTITY

The hip hop generation is not a monolithic group. One of the key variables that contributes to the hip hop generation's diversity is the class divide that has been aggravated within the African American community over the past thirty years. In *where we stand: class matters,* bell hooks puts it this way: "More and more, our nation is becoming class-segregated. The poor live with and among the poor—confined in gated communities without adequate shelter, food, or health care—the victims of predatory greed. More and more poor communities all over the country look like war zones, with boarded-up bombed-out buildings, with either the evidence of gunfire everywhere or the vacant silence of unsatisfied hunger."[2] This is the America where the hip hop generation has grown up. They have been estranged from their brothers and sisters as a result of the widening class divide within the African American community. Black flight followed white flight to the suburbs, and the result was a concentration of poverty in the inner cities that was overwhelming by black and brown.

This class divide within the African American community must be taken into account as we think about the diversity and divide within the hip hop generation. Many things bind the hip hop generation together, but the class divide lies at the root of what hip hop is and isn't. Hip hop comes out of and expresses a working-class ethic. As we seek to know them better and understand them, let us always remember the working-class foundation of hip hop, because this working-class ethic informs the hip hop lifestyle. On the one hand, we have at the core of the hip hop generation the aspiration for fulfilling the American dream from a working-class perspective. On the other hand, we have the black middle class who have embraced hip hop and sought success from a middle-class perspective while embracing the hard-working principles of hip hop.

Remember, when we talk about the hip hop generation, we are talking about young adults. The oldest hip hoppers were born in 1965. These are adults with jobs and children, and they are still listening to Ice Cube and Jay-Z. These are our children, our nephews and nieces. We have seen them grow up, some inside the church, but many of them outside the church. Their absence from the church has major social and financial repercussions for the church and the community. Young adults who are considered hip hop grew up hip hop. They grew up watching music, not listening to music. They grew up in a post–civil rights America.

These are some of their social markers, and these young adults look at the church, asking why they should come and sit with you when they feel at best that the church doesn't understand them, and at worst that the church has abandoned them. The hip hop generation's feelings of abandonment have led to a sense of cynicism on their part.

Whether working class or middle class, one thing the hip hop generation shares is that it tends to be cynical, as Cora Daniels points out. Although Daniels's work appears to speak more from a middle-class African American's perspective, her findings are applicable to working-class African Americans considered hip hop. In *Black Power Inc.: The New Voice of Success,* Daniels gives us a glimpse of these young, middle-class African Americans who have made it and are truly a part of hip hop culture.[3] They are cynical because they have seen the promises made during the civil rights era broken. They have worked hard in school and infiltrated corporate America, only to find that racism and what was once described as a glass ceiling have become a tiled ceiling. They are overwhelmed with their ability to sense racism.

They are a feeling generation, racism is what they feel and experience. Racism isn't something that they think they are obligated to prove with hard facts. Daniels has coined the term "working while Black" to describe what they experience in the work force. Lil Jon talks about the rejection they feel from a working-class perspective when they go and apply for a job; it screams, "Why bother?"[4] While middle-class hip hoppers are looking at the tiled ceiling, working-class African Americans aren't allowed on the ground floor. The obstacles they face in the work force inflict the pain of constant and blatant discrimination, with no legal recourse. Hip hop feels that America has no sense of ethical or moral sensitivity to the institutionalized racism, classism, and sexism that continue to produce false hope coupled with broken promises. For hip hoppers, this pain results in cynicism and shallow dreams—dreams of wealth and the gross American dream with little sense of civic responsibility, because civic America has forgotten about them.

Hip hoppers who have made it into the ranks of the middle class fight through their rage by working hard and overachieving. When they don't get invited to the party, they move beyond rage and throw their own party. To cite Daniels again, "This generation, itself, wants to be in charge."[5] They want to own their own company, control their own destiny. They don't want to depend on the system; they want to build their own system. An example of their owning and doing their own thing is reflected in how they make and own their art. Today's music moguls have their own companies. Their success strategies, based on hard work and ownership, are charted in *Hip-Hop Inc.: Success Strategies of the Rap Moguls*.[6] Hip hop moguls work with major record labels to iron out distribution deals while they own their art. These young stars are businessmen and businesswomen. They are just what Daniels found in her research: African Americans who want to be in charge, who are in charge, and who no longer depend on a system to reward them. They are their own system.

This characteristic says something to the church. Hip hoppers don't need the church to approve of or inform their religious worldview. They are constructing their own religious and spiritual world outside of church. When and if they come in the church, the church has to understand that they are used to having something to say, and they want to be heard. They will not be content to let the elders run them or run over them. They want to be involved in leadership. They are willing to be mentored, but not monitored! Their unwillingness to be bossed is linked to the historical legacy of African Americans' will to be free agents. This is nothing new; the question is, Will we respect their desire to be free as they define it? The church has to find a way to mentor them and love them while not discounting the elders. The church also has to be able to help them see that they need the elders. And more importantly, the elders have to be convinced that they need the hip hop generation in the church.

WE KNOW WHO WE BE!

The hip hop generation's understanding of who they are is deeply rooted in the context of their African American cultural heritage. A way of appealing to them is to tap into their reservoir of epic memory and to celebrate our African American culture with them. The hip hop generation is proud of their blackness and where they come from. Be they from the suburbs or the inner city, they celebrate their blackness. The generation before hip hop tried to cross over in the music industry and in corporate life. The hip hop generation has invited folk to come over to their side of life, and they invited others to come over on their terms. They are not willing to act differently because white folk are looking and listening in. Hip hoppers aren't going to change their look, walk, or talk because white people show up in the room. Hip hop proudly celebrates the working-class/ghetto culture. Hip hoppers write their songs about the ghetto. They dress ghetto, rap ghetto, dance ghetto, and if you don't like it, then that's your problem. Being black, according to Daniels, is a positive for this generation and the very source of their success. "The post–civil rights generation succeeds because they are Black. Their Blackness is what drives them and what pushes them, and ultimately it becomes their goal to succeed for the race that they are carrying. They want a new and different outcome, not the one they were handed—so they try new things."[7]

The new thing they are trying is simply being true to who they are and what they represent. When you listen to rap music, it is clear that the rapper, in many cases, is representing where he or she comes from. Rap and hip hop have a regional identity rooted in the community. Rappers mention the very street, the side of town, and the city they are representing. A fundamental element in hip hop is to represent your set, or where you are from. To be a real representative is a part of the test of authenticity that every hip hop artist must pass, and this realness is linked directly to their blackness. Even for those who aren't African American, their authenticity and credibility as a rap artist or their being a part of the hip hop community is measured by their ability to resonate with the African American experience and how African Americans have defined hip hop as a way of life. The hip hop generation leads from the point of blackness. Their being in charge and looking to those who are to be in charge is inextricably linked to this idea of blackness, freedom, ownership, and liberation.

Leaders who are hip hop are not your old-school leader. Hip hoppers want leaders who are transparent, honest, and willing to share their struggles and how they overcame. Hip hoppers' cynicism also feeds into their hermeneutic of suspicion. This means they don't trust at first sight. They inspect at first sight and have a wait-and-see attitude when it comes to those with whom they choose to share leadership. They want their leaders to speak from the heart and from experience.

What they look for in leaders says a lot about the type of preaching hip hoppers will be attracted to. They are a people of truth stories. The rappers who have longevity and success are those who use their personal story as community story that shares the truth in struggle and what struggle produces. This translates into preaching that is authentic, honest, revealing—rooted in story that is practical and relevant. It works not just on Sunday but also on Monday through Saturday. Preachers who are going to be successful with the hip hop generation will be preachers who reclaim the telling of the story—the old, old story and your story—as it relates to the hip hop generation's story, in their language. In summary, effective preaching to the hip hop generation is about truth, translation, and honesty. When you read Jason Barr's story, you will see that this pastor—who is over fifty—has reached the hip hop generation by being transparent as a preacher. He makes his testimony, past and present, a part of his preaching. As scary and risky as this can be, this is one way to reach this generation. As hip hoppers would put it, "Be real." They follow and support leaders who are honest and keep it real as they look for leaders in their elders and among themselves.

The leadership paradigm for this generation has shifted from that of their elders. Where their elders pretended or ignored the blemishes or sins of their leaders, hip hop embraces the tension of real-life faults and failings. The hip hop generation neither looks for nor needs the types of leaders that the former generation looked to and supported. Daniels says, "This generation is looking for leadership in all of us, every day."[8] They expect people to step up as individuals and lead from their centers of influence and power. They are not looking for leaders who are anointed by the press or an existing institution. They reward and respect indigenous leaders who have paid their dues in the community by service and a lifestyle that reflects their story. You find that in the hip hop nation, their leaders have come primarily from within or have been associated with the hip hop industry.

From Sister Soulja to Diddy, they have come from the industry. Even the elder statespersons who are connected with hip hop and seen as leaders by the hip hop generation fit the definition we have offered as being real and in touch with their struggle. This is one reason that hip hoppers are attracted to senior leaders like Sonia Sanchez, Assatta Shakur, Afeni Shakur, Nikki Giovanni, Louis

Farrakhan, and Ben Chavis Muhammad. These leaders are honest, they share their struggles, they aren't afraid of the system or powers that be, and they are intimately involved in and welcoming of the hip hop nation. These leaders understand the hip hop generation and they engage them in dialogue. They rebuke hip hoppers when it is called for, but it is done with respect and out of a love that is rooted in the hip hop community. These senior leaders don't use the press to lash out at hip hop, and they don't allow the press to use them as enemies of hip hop.

So the hip hop generation is not leaderless, as some have claimed. They have leaders, but their leaders lead differently than leaders who were a part of the civil rights generation. Bakari Kitwana has not only identified many of their leaders but has also helped us understand how they lead. Kitwana contends that the hip hop generation's leaders are more career-minded and less likely to be activist. Both Kitwana and Daniels point to the hip hop generation's embrace of careers over activism as one of the ways we can understand the type of leadership they offer. Kitwana puts it this way: "The deterrence to activism in our generation may have also inadvertently encouraged this generation to choose career over activism. Few hip-hop generationers can resist the omnipresent consumer culture."[9] The will and drive to succeed has moved them from a core of community service and activism, and I would add to this, their loss of the church as a center. The major influences for this generation are not the church and black civic organizations; they are hip hop and American capitalism. They aren't active members of the NAACP or the local African American church. The mass media and their peers have more influence on this generation, so they are shaping how they lead and how they see leadership. Kitwana writes, "Today the influence of these traditional purveyors of Black culture have largely diminished in the face of power and pervasive technological advances and corporate growth. Now media and entertainment such as pop music, film, and fashion are among the major forces transmitting culture to this generation of Black Americans."[10]

The church, civic organizations, and the like have lost their influence over this generation, and we need to repair this relationship so that we can be in touch with them. Only if we are in touch can we touch them. This is at the core of the concern from the elders in our community. As much as we critique hip hop, how can we gain influence with hip hop? How can we involve hip hoppers in civic organizations, or how do we help create or renew churches and civic organizations? How do we make sense of this type of leadership and behavior? If the church and civic organizations aren't willing to be renewed, they will forever be out of touch with hip hop. Hip hop has to be integrated and to some extent assimilated into the historic centers of African American life. Hip hoppers need to sit with the elders around common tables, and the elders need to hear them. But hip hop is not interested in coming to tables that are preset. They must be invited to be a part of the table setting, setting agendas and renewing our organizations.

BIG, LOUD, AND FAST: INNER-CITY YOUTH CULTURE

To see and understand the hip hop generation, their elders must turn to where hip hop is looking for a sense of identity and self-worth. The elders have to see hip hop as these young people see themselves, not as the elders want them to be. Their sense of identity is heavily influenced by youth culture. Kitwana says, "Today, more and more Black youth are turning to rap music, music videos, designer clothing, popular Black films, and television programs for values and identity."[11] So, if hip hop is turning to popular culture rather than the black church or civic organizations for identity formation, and if the elders want a glimpse of how hip hop defines itself, the elders have to tune in. Commercials, ESPN, video games, music television, and the like are defining the identity of the hip hop nation.

As we watch how this generation constructs its definition of self, we also see and hear how they like others to communicate with them. They like all things big; they like it loud, fast, full color—a multidimensional and physical experience. They live in a world of hyperstimulation. The elders tend to think about worship services as something linear and primarily auditory, with a printed bulletin. This reality begins to expose the divide between the generations. Something of how the hip hop culture sees and experiences the world needs to be infused into worship services. This doesn't mean we have to throw the baby out with the bath water, but it does point the church to changes that we need to consider. If hip hop lives in a three-dimensional world, then worship must at least be informed by that world. To some extent, some churches don't speak the language of the hip hop generation. Hip hop wants bold visual images that speak back to them; they want interaction; they want their body to be moved in an engagement with what is being taught. They embrace change and celebrate motion.

At the core of liking it big, fast, and loud is the inner-city, working-class identity that continues to inform hip hop. In the noise-filled environment of the streets, a sound arose from the rubble. It was the beat box of hip hop and the rappers who accompanied them. As the break dancers began to spin around on the pavement and went wild, the foundation of hip hop was being laid. In the inner city, sounds ring out throughout the night. Be it a siren, a gunshot, or simply people talking in the streets, you always hear noise. The inner city is also a place of movement, constant movement, fast-paced movement. The city is where big high-rise buildings, big buses, big stores, and big schools tower and rumble and sprawl as symbolic reminders of the vastness of city life. It is in this vast chasm of scale and class that hip hop began to evolve around the embrace of the style and feel of the city. The style and feel of urban life—more specifically inner-city, working-class urban life—shape and inform all that is hip hop.

HIP HOP IS HARD WORK

The ethos of hip hop is hard work. Rappers who make it work hard. When you read the stories of the greatest rappers who have survived over the years, you see a hard-working crew. In school lunchrooms across the country, you can witness students rapping. They have worked hard on their lyrics. They have constructed a flowing story in rhyme. A good story is hard enough to write, but to put it in rhyme makes it twice as hard. They test their material in front of their peers. The work put in will show up now. The two rappers step to each other, and the battle ensues. It is a battle that reflects hard work and preparation, in which the audience has the privilege of participating. This is hip hop: hard, in-your-face work. Those who are pure hip hoppers tend to be workaholics. They love what they do, and they do it with passion, commitment, and a drive to succeed. Rappers, beat makers, DJs, dancers, fashion designers, graffiti artists, and those who make up the hip hop nation spend hours at their craft. As William J. Wilson has found in his research, traditional forms of work have disappeared from the inner city, but this has not stopped young people from working.[12] They continue to put in long hours doing what they do—that is hip hop.

From their music to their lifestyle, they work. The hip hop generation has tried to turn work into play. Or one could say what many observe: play is a form of work for the hip hop generation. They work on their rap and their hoop game. Todd Boyd has shown the tie between hip hop and basketball.[13] Their work on the court is another expression of the work ethic that is a part of hip hop. Robin D. G. Kelley put it this way, "Increasingly, young people have tried to turn play into an alternative to unfulfilling wage labor. Basketball, for black males at least, not only embodies dreams of success and possible escape from the ghetto. In a growing number of communities pickup games are played for more money."[14]

Not only are they playing pickup games for money; they are battling in ciphers as they rap face-offs for money. This is work, and the rappers who make it on the local or national scene work even harder to stay afloat in a very competitive multibillion-dollar hip hop industry. To survive in the hip hop industry, they have to understand struggle and hard work. The fact that hip hoppers are hard workers goes against what some may have thought it meant to be a nigga. They may not do what mainstream America considers as typical work, but they are working. They spend hours working at video games, perfecting their skills as they compete with their coworkers.

This too has implications for the church. Hip hoppers don't want to come to church to sit down and wait to be involved in the life, work, and ministry of the church. They are used to spending hours working. They are ready and prepared to work. Church rules that you have to be a member for a minimum period of time before you can lead or serve is a sure way to discourage hip hoppers from coming to church. Churches have to find ways to involve them, develop them, disciple them, and thrust them into service. This doesn't mean that they have to be on the deacon board or steward board in the first year of membership, but it does mean that a church that wants to attract and keep hip hoppers has to think prayerfully and objectively about the doors to ministry. Are the doors closed or open? How hard is it to break into leadership when a young person has something to offer? Are there opportunities and structures to develop new and relevant ministries with young leaders immediately? We must remember that hip hop is not used to waiting. This is the generation of fast food, fast cars, and fast money. What is the response time of your church?

REDEFINING WORDS: EMBRACING RACE, TENSION WITH SEX

As much as hip hop is about work—and it is—this working image is an image and work ethic that is tied to their nigga identity. Hip hop projects and sees itself as hard niggas. For hip hop, to be a nigga is a good thing. For the hip hop generation, the word *nigga* is at the center of the identity they embrace. Their elders didn't take the word positively, but this generation does. Tupac intentionally redefined the word; for him, the word meant never ignorant, getting goals accomplished.[15] It is important to embrace the nigga attitude if you want to understand the hip hop generation and how they see the world. Boyd helps us here when he says, "The modern-day 'nigga,' having come to prominence through several cultural arenas including rap music, African American cinema, and professional sports, equally deifies aspects of mainstream white culture, as well as the at times restrictive dimensions of status quo Black culture. Ultimately the defining characteristic of the modern-day nigga is class, as opposed to what used to be exclusively race."[16] The working-class nuances of *nigga* have extended its identity-framing powers into middle-class identities for hip hop as both working- and middle-class hip hoppers embrace the term along with its identity construction.

The nigga identity signifies a break from the past use of the word and the previous generations' definition of what it means to be black or African American. Boyd charts this move: old-school definitions of blackness have vanished; what has emerged is the new nigga. This is an embrace of blackness at an earthy level. It rejects former notions of success as equated with whiteness and embraces a rebellious nature that fights against the total assimilation of young African Americans into mainstream white culture. As much as the hip hop generation seeks success in capitalistic terms, they will be niggas as they do it. They will hold on to what the streets taught them. They will embrace their ghettocentric cultural values.

If you study the life and times of Shawn Carter, also known as Jay-Z, the president of Def Jam Records, you find that throughout his meteoric rise to fame he cites his growing up in the Marcey Projects in New York as the key to his success. The hustla image for Jay-Z and artists like Cassidy or Rick Ross are all about being hustlas or hard-workers from a working-class perspective that is linked back to the ghetto. Even hip hoppers who aren't a part of the ghetto reality still cling to the truth, grit, struggle, and hard work of the ghetto. They are polished in a ghetto way. They wear clothes that match (very African American) but are too big for them. They wear jewelry around their necks, in their ears, and in their mouths. A grille, or a plate of gold to cover the teeth, is a standard part of their attire. Sports shoes or mountain boots are standard dress-up gear. Pants hanging down with a button-up shirt without a tie is "fly".

The church has to ask, How do we become more ghetto? How can we make Jesus speak to niggas? How can we effectively address the sociological identity construct of young African Americans who see themselves as niggas? A church that is too polished, too smooth, not improvisational, doesn't move at a pace that sustains attention, speaks one language, is focused on auditory and not multisensory worship, is a church that is saying to hip hop, *We don't want you here.* Our sign may read "All are welcome," but the question is, does hip hop feel welcomed when it comes to church? Is hip hop banned in your church? Is hip hop banned in the sense that the church has done very little if anything to intentionally integrate the hip hop nation into the active witness of the church every Sunday and throughout the week?

As much as hip hop is rooted in a new nigga image, there is also the role of women in hip hop that is caught in the tension of the "B" word and the "F" word. In the context of hip hop, a B—— can be either positive or negative. To understand the word and its meaning, the hearer must analyze the author's intent, as understood by the hearer. Let me put it this way: Those who are hip hop struggle with the sexism in hip hop, and their struggle is felt in the music and the hip hop nation. There isn't unanimity when it comes to issues of sexism and misogyny in hip hop.

Joan Morgan has done the best work I have found to date in dealing with the tension of being a female and a member of the hip hop nation and dealing with the sexism and misogyny in hip hop culture. In *When Chickenheads Come Home to Roost: My Life as a Hip-Hop Feminist,* Morgan suggests that the term *nigga* and the "B" word are a reflection of the pain in the hip hop nation. She writes, "It's extremely telling that men who can only see us as 'bitches' and 'hos' refer to themselves only as 'niggas.'"[17] Morgan argues that at the heart of the "B" word and the "H" word are the brokenness and pain in the hip hop nation. The men who are a part of the hip hop nation have been socialized and indoctrinated to think that brown women and their brothers are the enemy. In many instances, they miss the real culprit of the continuing legacy of racism. In her work, Morgan also points to the fact that some women in the culture don't demand respect and instead embrace the negative connotations and denotations of the "B" word. In the end, Morgan argues that the tension around this language needs to be embraced by the hip hop community and dealt with. She suggests that hip hop is the place where authentic dialogue around these issues can and should take place.

Despite the extent that the "B" word is a part of the hip hop lexicon, there is no agreement about its role, usage, and informing of who the community is. The connotation of the word and the image of a B—— can be one of power and prowess or one of pain and exploitation. The church has to realize that the "B" word and image is a part of hip hop culture. Therefore the church must listen to how the word and image is being used by an artist or a part of the hip hop community before the church passes judgment. If the church hopes to ever understand hip hop, it must enter into hip hop's struggle with its language. Hip hop thrives on creating words that help them understand, redefine, and shape their world. As much as hip hop uses the "N" word, the "B" word, and the "F" word, there is also the use of *brotha* and *sista* in hip hop. At the concerts I attend, the artists refer to the crowd as *fam*. The hip hop nation sees itself as a family. The art that forms the foundation for the culture becomes a rallying point that brings the family together. There are arguments over words and over their use, but there is unanimity that hip hop is a family, a nation, one that hip hoppers belong to proudly.

Where the church was once that place of family and gathering, hip hop is fast becoming today's alternative. Hip hop culture brings young people together. They come together to have family love and family fights. Although some churches invite them in and then develop a segregated service for them, or reach out to them one Sunday a month, what they want is to be a part of the larger family every day of the week. They want to be integrated into the life of the church and the mainstream African American community. As we said earlier, hip hop also wants to have something to say about how this integration is to take place, but they want to be a part of the world that their elders have developed. The elders have to listen and see this chapter as only a glimpse of this complex and diverse group of young African Americans who want to be a part of the church of Jesus Christ. Once we begin to sit and share stories, something will happen. Our perceptions of each other will change. We will learn from each other and begin to grow.

This chapter's sketch of the hip hop generation is not the final word on who our young people are becoming. It is a first word that is meant to give us a snapshot, not a full-length feature. The purpose of this chapter has been to introduce some of the trends and influences we see in hip hop culture. After reading this chapter, it is incumbent upon church leadership to test the suggestions in this chapter against what they see in their local situations. There will be varying degrees of resonance between what we see in the general population of the hip hop nation and what you see in your church and community. To find out more, talk to your hip hop community about what you have read. Have them critique the way we have defined them and talk about how they would define themselves. To get to know them better will not be a result of your reading a book, but rather of your talking to them. This chapter and this book are primarily intended to stimulate a dialogue between the elders of the church and hip hop. We have to be willing to talk face to face as well as touch the culture.

As we move to the next chapter, we find that the children of the hip hop nation are even more removed from the church than are their mothers and fathers. The children of the hip hop nation, or what I like to call hip hop squared, will be even more demanding than the previous generation that the church make changes in the way we have done what we have done. They grew up completely in the high days of hip hop. We now move to looking at hip hop squared, and we engage in a futuring exercise that we hope will be helpful in reaching out to our young adults and their children.

NOTES

1. Bakari Kitwana, *The Hip Hop Generation: Young Blacks and the Crisis in African-American Culture* (New York: Basic Civitas Books, 2002), xiii.
2. bell hooks, *where we stand: class matters* (New York: Routledge, 2000), 2.
3. Cora Daniels, *Black Power Inc.: The New Voice of Success* (Hoboken, N.J.: John Wiley, 2004).
4. Lil Jon, "Stop F——in Wit Me," *Crunk Juice*, CD (TVT Records, 2004).
5. Daniels, 54.
6. Richard Oliver and Tim Leffel, *Hip-Hop Inc.: Success Strategies of the Rap Moguls* (New York: Thunder's Mouth Press, 2006).
7. Daniels, 119.
8. Ibid., 135.
9. Kitwana, 154.
10. Ibid., 7.
11. Ibid., 9.
12. William J. Wilson, *When Work Disappears: The World of the New Urban Poor* (New York: Alfred A. Knopf, 1996).
13. Todd Boyd, *Young, Black, Rich, and Famous: The Rise of the NBA, the Hip Hop Invasion, and the Transformation of American Culture* (New York: Doubleday, 2003).
14. Robin D. G. Kelley, *Yo' Mama's DisFUNKtional! Fighting the Culture Wars in Urban America* (Boston: Beacon, 1997), 53.
15. Michael Eric Dyson, *Holler If You Hear Me: Searching for Tupac Shakur* (New York: Basic Civitas Books, 2002), 144.
16. Todd Boyd, *Am I Black Enough for You? Popular Culture from the 'Hood and Beyond* (Bloomington: Indiana University Press, 1997), 31.
17. Joan Morgan, *When Chickenheads Come Home to Roost: My Life as a Hip-Hop Feminist* (New York: Simon & Schuster, 1999), 7.

CHAPTER 3
MY BABY'S MOMMA: HIP HOP^2, THE BABIES OF THE HIP HOP GENERATION

"Take heed that you do not despise one of these little ones, for I say to you that in heaven their angels always see the face of My Father who is in heaven."

—Matthew 18:10 NKJV

It was a Friday night, and once again I was on my way to DJ a gig. Tonight I had been invited to DJ a lock-in for the youth of a church. I arrived at the church early to find one car in the parking lot. A lady and her daughters were there, and they, like I, were waiting to enter. I am always surprised by how empty church parking lots can feel and appear on days other than Sunday. About thirty minutes later, an elderly gentleman arrived, and he let us in. My assistant and I unloaded equipment, got our set-up together, and tested the sound system. Everything was fine, so we sat back and waited for the youth and adults to arrive. Around 6:30 p.m., people began to flow slowly into the basement of the church. As the small crowd began to form, it became obvious that some of the kids knew each other while others were outside of the network of family and friends. As we approached 7 p.m., the youth pastor called for the youth to circle up and to introduce themselves by giving their name, grade in school, the school they attended, and their church home. As the youth pastor outlined the things he wanted the kids to share during introductions, at first glance there appeared to be nothing wrong with his request. I found myself in the circle, the only other adult, and I was anxiously waiting to hear from the kids.

The introductions began, and we were moving around the circle smoothly. The church kids rattled off their church name, and many announced who their pastor was. As the introductions proceeded, I began to see a few kids who were anxious about their turn. They put their heads down as if they were searching for answers to the request from the youth pastor. These kids were at the tail end of the circle; I could only imagine that they were the shy kids who didn't like to speak in public. As their turn got closer, you could almost feel their hesitation and reservation. Now it was their turn to introduce themselves: name, grade, school—then their heads dropped as they mumbled, "I don't have a church home yet." The last answer, about not having a church home, was spoken in shame and pain. These were the kids who weren't a part of the family and friends network. They were inside a building of which they didn't feel a part. These were kids who had walked to the lock-in. After the "nonchurch" kids finished their introductions, with their heads down, the youth pastor began his evangelistic appeal. In his loud, loving, preacher's voice he spoke of how the church kids needed to reach out to "these" unchurched kids. He echoed to the church kids that this was an opportunity to witness to nonchurched, "community kids." He wanted the church kids to act like Christians tonight, so this behavior might in turn lead some of the "community kids" to become Christians.

As the youth pastor made his appeal, in love and with sincerity, the room was silent. The nonchurch kids had been singled out. They had been called out, as it were. Everyone in the circle, including me, was looking at them. The youth pastor wasn't doing a bad thing, and he wasn't trying to single them out—he was trying to reach out. But in his sincere attempt to *reach* out, he had *put* out the unchurched kids. They were in the circle but not of the circle. It was as if a red mark had been placed on their foreheads. Where could they hide? What could they say? What could they do?

This scene speaks to the divide that is developing within the African American community. It is a divide that is rooted in class, a divide between the African American church and the larger, working-class African American community. It is a divide that many don't want to talk about, but it is one we can't ignore. Kids around many African

American churches don't feel comfortable or welcomed in those churches. As much as the church has a heart and love for them, we have to be retrained as to how to reach them, affirm them, welcome them, and integrate them and their culture into the church. These are the kids of what we will call hip hop squared—hip hop^2.

CHURCH KIDS VERSUS COMMUNITY KIDS

At the root of this problem is the divide between African American churches whose buildings are in working-class communities and whose financial support comes from middle-class African Americans who commute to church. Middle-class, bourgeoisie values permeate the church as middle-class blacks have done all they can to not be considered "ghetto." The class consciousness of the church is linked to church membership as well, and the status of class and church membership is extended to youth in the church. The church has made a distinction between the church kids versus the community kids. The kids who are not formal members of the church are considered outside of the church, and the church is not responsible or liable for their behavior or status. This divide is exacerbated when church leaders speak of the divide without speaking to the divide. Labeling kids as outside versus inside points to the challenge the church will have when it comes to reaching the children of the hip hop generation.

At the church lock-in, as the night went on the community kids appeared to be under surveillance by the church leaders. When the church kids were being rude and disrespectful, their behavior was noticed before it was obvious, but they weren't put in check. But as the community kids were getting into the music, getting loud and very demonstrative, they were quickly put in check. The community kids were affirming my DJing and the lecture I gave about the history of hip hop. Their affirmation was boisterous; they were acting out what they were hearing. As I gave my evening lecture, the youth pastor came and stood by the community kids and gave them the evil eye. On the other side of the room the church kids weren't as engaged and were yelling out inappropriate comments. The church kids' behavior was tolerated, but the community kids' behavior was monitored. The community kids were reflecting the music and the environment they come from. They embraced their ghetto image in a healthy way. For churches, especially churches that see themselves as respectable, middle-class bastions, this type of ghetto behavior is deplorable. This tension between ghetto and nonghetto behavior was even more evident as the night progressed. The youth pastor and the adult chaperones made it clear that there was not going to be any ghetto behavior. They walked up to the community kids and make corrections on the spot.

As my lecture ended and the music resumed, the community kids were once again rebuked for the way they were dancing. They weren't doing anything wrong. To put it simply, they were having a good time. They were jumping around and dancing the way kids tend to do at all the dances I DJ. But on this occasion the youth pastor—who appeared to be out of touch with hip hop culture—was dismissive of their actions and saw fit to correct them. The church kids, who were on the other side of the room, were doing their own nasty thing, but they weren't as loud as the community kids, and their suggestive dancing was ignored. While the community kids' jumping around and going hyphy, or wild, was brought under submission, the church kids were left alone. The lines of demarcation were drawn. The community kids were marked from the beginning of the evening, and they were outlawed. I don't know if the church kids acted as a witness to the community kids. I wonder what the community kids thought of the youth pastor and me. I don't know what kind of witness I was. I never came to their defense or even tried to bring attention to what I saw going on. If anything, I tried to listen to kids' requests and play the music they wanted to hear (clean, edited versions of hip hop), but that is as far as my witness went.

What does it mean to be a witness to hip hop squared, those who live in the community but don't attend churches in their community? Are they us? Are we them? How serious is the divide between us and them? When did the African American church start using "us" and "them" when it comes to other black people?

As I packed up my equipment at the end of my set, the community kids were the first to affirm my DJing and volunteered to help me. They told me I had done a good job. One young lady came up to me and said, "I had brought some CDs, but you had it." I was out of there, but the event lingered in my mind as I drove home. My assistant and I mulled over the events of the night, and this issue of church kids versus community kids kept creeping back into our conversation. This divide between church and community—what is it all about? When I got home, I woke up my wife at 3 a.m. to talk to her about what I had experienced. The more we talked, the more it appeared that we were talking in circles: the same critique I had of the church I had just left could be applied to the church that my wife and I attended and where we also worked with youth and young adults. The more we talked, the more we realized that this divide had been noticeable in the churches I had pastored and served over the last fifteen years. This divide goes back almost a generation.

The youth pastor at the church I had just left wasn't a bad guy; he was me, and I was he. We were products of an African American community that has experienced a divide—a divide based on class and status, a divide based on hip hop and non-hip hop. Some churches are disconnected from the very communities in which their buildings take up major real estate. They are also divided in the sense that they not only don't know about hip hop and the children of hip hop, but many even appear to not want to know. Many are content to invite people like me in for the one-day or half-day workshop—which most of the elders don't attend—and then think they have done their part. The problem is much bigger than a dance or a one-day workshop. The problem is about the future of the African American church and the health and wholeness of the African American community. As we continue to divide ourselves, we only increase the gap, while the community is waiting for the church to have a great coming-out party that brings us together again. When we talk about leading change in the church (chapter 4), we will offer some ideas about how the church might deal with these issues.

CHAPTER 3

HIP HOP^2

If the African American church doesn't address the divide between working class and middle class, hip hop and non-hip hop, the church will find itself out of touch with the children of the hip hop generation and the masses of working-class African Americans. The babies of the hip hop generation, hip hop^2 or hip hop squared, are those born from 1987 to 2007. This next generation of hip hoppers differs from their parents in several ways. One of the first and most glaring differences between the hip hop generation and hip hop^2 is that hip hop^2 is farther removed from the African American church than their parents were. Over the past twenty years, inner-city America has been victimized by a lack of family-sustaining employment, poor public education, and an absence of community support for inner-city residents, primarily from their middle-class brothers and sisters. The product of this family fallout has been a spiral of poor families without a sustained male presence. This social crisis is producing a permanent underclass and a burgeoning divide between the African American middle and working classes.

The work of sociologist William J. Wilson, along with that of cultural critics bell hooks and Michael Eric Dyson, will inform the discussion in this chapter. The works of these scholars point to the class divide that will be fully realized during the lifetime of the hip-hop-squared generation. We call attention to this problem with the hope of empowering the church to realize the challenge of reaching hip hop squared while pointing to possible strategies in reaching out and up to right the wrongs that are speaking death on our families and children.

THE FOUNDATION OF THE DIVIDE

When William J. Wilson published *The Declining Significance of Race* in 1978, it set off a fire storm.[1] The title of the book was misleading, because it implied that race and racism were becoming less significant in America. The critique of the book revolved around the misleading title, and many of Wilson's critics never moved beyond the title to deal with the substance and veracity of his argument. Twenty years later, bell hooks published *where we stand: class matters.*[2] When you read Wilson's book along with hooks's book, you find amazing agreement. What both Wilson and hooks say is that America is becoming a place where *class* is the most critical dividing line when it comes to life chances. Neither hooks nor Wilson argues that racism or race issues have disappeared from the American landscape or lessened in their importance. They both would agree that race, racism, and sexism are still huge issues, and they would also agree that class segregation plagues America. The class divide is not limited to white America; hooks and Wilson would say this class divide is at the center of the crisis in black America. African Americans are divided along class lines more than ever, and this divide cuts through the church too, while at the same time the church stands in the middle of the divide and is the hope for bridging it. A geographical divide aggravates this class divide as well, because middle-class African Americans have moved out of the inner city and into the suburbs. White flight and black flight use the same freeways to flee the inner city.

When the civil rights movement came to an end, many middle-class African Americans took the train uptown and out of town and left their brothers and sisters behind as they sang "Movin' on Up" from *The Jeffersons.* What was left was a high concentration of inner-city communities filled with African Americans who would eventually be labeled as the new working poor. The working poor are people who work hard every day, but because their wages hover around the minimum wage they are still trapped in poverty. The new world of black working poor evolved into communities without the balance of a middle-class presence. As the middle class left inner-city communities and the global service economy began to take shape, work also disappeared from these communities. And as the middle class moved out, their dollars, banks, restaurants, stores, and so on also moved. Social institutions were weakened, and the church was left holding the bag. "The bag" consisted of a religious institution that had once been the center of the community but now sat in the middle of abandoned urban neighborhoods with parking lots that had to be monitored by security guards. The churches' core membership and supporters had moved, and they were finding it hard to relate to those who were left in the community.

Who was left in the community? Along comes a generation of young African Americans, working-class, hardcore, inner-city youths that the church was not equipped or ready to handle. C. Eric Lincoln put it best when he said, "The demographic movement of middle-income blacks out of the inner city areas and into residential parts of the cities, older suburbs, or into newly created black suburbs, has meant a growing physical and social isolation of the black poor. For example, since the 1960s, 48 percent of the black population of Atlanta has moved out of the central city into surrounding counties."[3] This shift within the African American community, with the middle class and working class being separated by sociogeographic barriers, is the world of hip hop squared. It is a world untouched by their brothers and sisters who have exchanged public school for private school. Urban hip hop^2 have not had contact with the affluent African Americans who could serve as partners as they try to make the American dream a reality. The inner city has become a world of isolation and dislocation, and the African American churches and many of their supporters are out of touch with the working-class, inner-city child who represents hip hop squared.

This distance and the power of hip hop in both sectors of the African American community—middle class and working class—in many ways explains why hip hop has been so influential. It may also explain how we can bring the community together again. For both working-class and middle-class African Americans, hip hop has helped define what it means to be black across class lines and across the sociogeographic barrier. The church can learn something from hip hop when it comes to touching hip hop squared: namely, they are searching for an ethnic identity. This identity is being broadly defined by hip hop, but it can be specifically defined by a local church or cluster of churches that share something in common. The church can learn from hip hop how hip hop squared understand themselves in relation to African American community identity. What does hip hop know that the African American church doesn't know or has forgotten? At the core of hip hop is African American culture, which celebrates the way we walk, talk, and act. Hip hop is unapologetic when it comes to defining what it means to be black. Churches and church leaders may or may not agree with how they are defining blackness, but one must admit that they are trying to define blackness. Maybe the church can embrace a definition of blackness and serve as a rallying point to reach out to the hip hop generation. Maybe the church could engage in dialogue with hip hop and its definition of blackness with a definition from the church that is biblical and includes working-class and middle-class values.

In many churches, class identity and class status take precedence over ethnic identity. It is very difficult for a pastor and the church leaders to build a mass church made up equally of persons from the working, middle, and upper classes. But the ever-increasing importance of class-based identity in black churches is antithetical to the hip hop ethos. The reality is that upper-class, middle-class, and working-class African Americans all embrace hip hop. When you go to hip hop concerts, you see kids and young adults from all walks of black life. Class status is second to that of being hip hop. Hip hop has found a way to reach across class lines and develop a mass audience; it has done what the church has found great difficulty in trying to do. The church can learn from hip hop, and by learning and embracing hip hop culture the church can bridge the divide within the African American community. The link that hip hop has made is their embracing of the core ethic of African American culture in its contemporary state. Hip hop isn't stuck in the past. Hip hop has embraced the evolution and development of African American culture and art as it continues to mature in hip hop culture.

Hip hop appeals to what unites African Americans as a minority group. Minority status is based on the fact that a group of people has been singled out and experiences collective discrimination based on being members of that group. African Americans, regardless of class status, still experience racial discrimination in America. There is still an African American culture that is alive and well in the inner city and the suburbs. Hip hop takes African American minority status, along with the key elements of African American culture, and uses them to advance hip hop culture. As formally educated as a hip hopper might be, he or she maintains fluency in Ebonics. Hip hoppers celebrate being black and all that it means regardless of what someone outside the community may think about them. If the African American church goes back to its historical roots, it will find that this is what made the African American church unique. It developed and celebrated a faith that spoke against the dominant culture, and African American preachers and choirs did it the black way.

Some readers may be asking, What is the black way? I point you to Styles P's song "I'm Black" or Cornel West's *Sketches of My Culture.*[4] If, after listening to Cornel West and Styles P, you are still unclear on what it means to be black, go to your family barbecue or to a historically black college or university homecoming. Go to your home church in Alabama or Mississippi. Watch the movies *The Color Purple, A Raisin in the Sun,* and *Brown Sugar.* If what it means to be black is still fuzzy, read Richard Wright, Gwendolyn Brooks, J. California Cooper, and Bebe Moore Campbell. There is something to this notion of what it means to be black, and if you are truly black you know what it is. You can taste it in the sweet potato pie, and you can hear it in our preachers and choirs.

As we consider the concept of what it means to be black, we have to once again return to the divide within the African American experience. Michael Eric Dyson shed light on this divide within the African American community as he neatly defined two broad categories of African Americans in *Is Bill Cosby Right? Or Has the Black Middle Class Lost Its Mind?* The one group he has labeled the Afristocracy and the other group the Ghettocracy. According to Dyson, the Afristocracy are "upper middle-class blacks and black elite who rain down fire and brimstone upon poor blacks for their deviance and pathology, and for their lack of couth and culture."[5] In the Afristocracy, Dyson includes the African American church. He defines the Ghettocracy as "the black poor...the desperately unemployed and underemployed, those trapped in underground economies, and those working poor folk who slave in menial jobs at the edge of the economy."[6] Dyson goes on to expose the tension between these two groups. He contends that many of those in the Afristocracy once were poor and black, but now that they have "arrived" the question is whether they have forgotten where they came from (the Ghettocracy). Dyson calls for the Afristocracy to look on their brothers and sisters trapped in poverty not with contempt but with love and understanding. The questions for the black church, which is a part of the Afristocracy, are, How do we love our brothers and sisters who are not among us or with us? How do we reach up and out with love and not condemnation?

An example of the depth of the divide is was brought home to me again recently. An editorial by attorney Joe Hopkins in a local black weekly newspaper, *The Pasadena Journal,* attacked hip hop and the entire hip hop generation. The blanket critique of all that is hip hop included the work many churches are doing to try to reach hip hoppers.[7] In the editorial, the writer painted hip hop as the downfall of African American culture and civility. The editorial appeared to leave little if any room for a discussion about hip hop or for the members of the Ghettocracy who produce it and are proud of it. Hopkins had obviously not listened to much rap music, and he was not even willing to entertain that there was some good rap. To him, it was all bad.

Whether one agrees with Hopkins or not, the fact remains that he is a member of the very Afristocracy that Dyson describes, and Hopkins is a living example of the divide within the African American community. He in many ways represents what I find as I go to talk to churches about hip hop—hostile crowds who by and large haven't engaged the breadth and depth of hip hop culture. We have to speak to this divide, or we will not reach hip hop^2, who are very much rooted in the Ghettocracy of the African American community and are not in our churches. If we are to reach them, we will have to find ways to embrace and integrate parts of their culture into the life of the church. I firmly believe that while some churches and church leaders may not know much about hip hop or hip hop culture, this ignorance says little about their compassion and desire to reach the hip hop generation and to include hip hop squared. Churches want to reach out to both the hip hop generation and hip hop squared.

PUT YA' HANDS UP: SAY YEAH

If churches want to move beyond critique to reaching out to hip hop and hip hop squared, they will have to understand that hip hop^2 grew up in a world of cable television, Internet, video music, and video games. These young people will feel that a paced and regimented worship service drags along, and it will not interest them. The way we have done preaching in the past will not excite them. If we can't touch their culture and excite all of their senses, we lose them. Like the video game industry, they are looking for the newest, the hottest, and the greatest thing this year as they look forward to next year. They like unpredictable, immediately responsive experiences that speak to all senses. A predictable worship service, rooted in a traditional liturgy, will not enlist them, excite them, attract them, or keep them.

Like the video games and music videos they watch, the worship they are looking for has to be moving. It has to be a worship that involves them as active participants. Hip hop calls on the audience to be intimately involved as active participants in all that it does. This isn't far removed from what the African American church has always done: the church has had a tradition of call and response. The difference now is that hip hop^2 wants to be more demonstrative. They want instruction and engagement that leads to or encourages excitement and energy. Hip hop squared is about energy, passion, and inclusion. To call them to participate in something that doesn't reflect them or their culture will only turn them off. They are not going to be active, supportive participants in a cultural expression rooted in past methods, whether monologue or dialogue. They want a cultural mirror that reflects them, even as they are willing to be corrected, instructed, and presented with truth.

Hip hop squared wants the church to be a little ghetto, but being ghetto is the one thing that most middle-class African Americans and our churches have run away from. If you think about it, the ghetto image speaks not only to the class divide but also to hip hop squared. Hip hop^2 is a class-based, working-class community primarily made up of kids and young adults outside the middle-class African American church. They feel comfortable with cultural expressions rooted in their experience—which is the ghetto, in both a negative and a positive sense. If they walk into a church that condemns their culture and way of life, it is in essence condemning them. Everybody wants to walk into a church that embraces and affirms them. This starts with culture. The African American church must embrace the culture of the ghetto and make it a part of who we are.

What will a church that is a little ghetto look like? It will look a lot like our churches looked in their inception. It will be a church rooted in African American expressions of our complete cultural heritage. It not only will sing contemporary praise songs but also will go back and sing songs that sound and feel like hip hop. It will be a church conscious of the need to include expressions of the African American community that cut across class lines and intentionally include both the Afristocracy and the Ghettocracy. It will be a church that sits down on Sunday morning and asks, Who isn't here? This is not a question about which members didn't show up for worship, but rather a question that asks who from the broader African American community is absent. Are Sequeatha and Ramel in worship? You know them: they live in the subsidized housing that the church manages. They are the ones we speak to as we leave church, while they are walking by the very church they could be attending. If the African American church continues to embrace an ethos that speaks of

Afristocracy values and doesn't engage ghetto culture with empathy and objectivity, we will never become the church we could become.

I know the image of ghetto behavior is hard for us. I am a member of the Afristocracy: my wife and I both hold doctoral degrees; we attend First African Methodist Episcopal Church in Los Angeles. I am writing from everyday experience. This is hard work. I too hear the music and see the behavior and at first glance I am repulsed by it, but I have to force myself to move beyond my initial feelings and look deeper. The questions I constantly ask myself are, How do I touch what I haven't listened to? How do I teach and preach to what I have condemned? How do I feel what they feel? How can I grow closer to them? How do I deal with my tendencies to be judgmental and elitist? How can I get close enough to my brothers and sisters so that we can have a mutual conversation? How can we reconnect so that we can better understand each other? I offer these questions to the African American church as we seek to reach out to hip hop^2. This young generation is waiting on us.

In the words of the Pointer Sisters, "We Are Family." It is time for a family reunion, and what better place than the church! Every family reunion ends up at the home church. We all sit together, the Ph.D.s and the GEDs. We sit down together, and we are recognized as one family. When it comes to hip hop squared, we have to claim them as part of our family. We have to invite them to the reunion at the local church and empower them to have a say in how the reunion takes place. We have to have some of their music, and we can't outlaw the way they dress, talk, walk, and act. If they are us and we are them, we are reflected in each other. In some cases, hip hop squared may have remembered what those of us from the Afristocracy may have forgotten.

As the reunion takes place, the African American community will be re-membered, or put back together again. The divide will be diminished at each gathering. We will know each other by name and not be defined by class status or generational location. The divide between the civil rights generation and the hip hop generation will be closed, and we will stand together to fight the battles that lie ahead. Now the only question that remains is, Who will send out the invitations to the reunion? The sign in front of the church, "All Welcomed," isn't enough. To get folk to the reunion we are going to have to reconnect. We are going to have to make phone calls, knock on doors, speak and listen to each other. Only when folk know there is a place for them at the reunion will they come. So I ask, What is the date for the reunion?

NOTES

1. William J. Wilson, *The Declining Significance of Race: Blacks and Changing American Institutions* (Chicago: University of Chicago Press, 1978).
2. bell hooks, *where we stand: class matters* (New York: Routledge, 2000).
3. C. Eric Lincoln and Lawrence H. Mamiya, *The Black Church in the African American Experience* (Durham, N.C.: Duke University Press, 1990), 384.
4. Styles P, "I'm Black," *Time Is Money,* CD (Ruff Ryders Records, 2005); Cornel West, *Sketches of My Culture,* CD (Artemis Records, 2001).
5. Michael Dyson, *Is Bill Cosby Right? Or Has the Black Middle Class Lost Its Mind?* (New York: Basic Civitas Books, 2005), xiii.
6. Ibid., xiv.
7. Joe Hopkins, editorial, *The Pasadena Journal,* August 31, 2006, http://www.pasadenajournal.com.

CHAPTER 4
A CHARGE TO KEEP I HAVE: INSTITUTIONAL BARRIERS TO REACHING THE HIP HOP GENERATION

"Go therefore and make disciples of all the nations, baptizing them in the name of the Father and of the Son and of the Holy Spirit, teaching them to observe all things that I have commanded you; and lo, I am with you always, even to the end of the age." Amen.

—Matthew 28:19-20 NKJV

A church that is unwilling to embrace change is a church that will not reach the hip hop generation. This is a strong statement, but I stand by it. Churches and church leaders that hope to reach the hip hop generation will have to embrace an ethic of biblically based change. I would even say that if a church is to be true to the Great Commission to make disciples of all nations, which includes the hip hop nation, it will have to make changes. In the end, the church has to be confronted with its witness as it relates to evangelism and the making of disciples of the hip hop nation. It is really this simple. The church has to deal honestly with the response or lack thereof—who is coming or not coming down the aisle at the end of the sermon. If the hip hop generation isn't present in the worship service, they can't respond to the preached word. If the church doesn't preach a word that they can hear and understand, they may come, but they will not stay and become disciples. The change that the church will have to pray about and make first asks, How will we take the timeless eternal message of salvation and discipleship and package it in contemporary culture?

In this chapter, I do not intend to dictate what changes churches need to make. Instead, I will raise the questions churches need to think about as we relate to change and reaching the hip hop generation. At the core of the process is the question of how the church understands evangelism and its evangelistic program. I like the way William J. Abraham defines evangelism: as initiation into the kingdom of God. For Abraham, evangelism is not simply the proclamation of the word or social programs that help the poor. Rather, evangelism extends the making of disciples.[1] In Matthew 28:19-20, Jesus made the point that as we go out to share the word and be a witness, our work doesn't stop there. He made clear that the church is to teach and make disciples of those they are called to evangelize. Therefore, inherent in the definition and description of evangelism is the component of discipleship.

We can't stop at the definition given to us by Abraham, though, because in the African American tradition we have a deep and rich definition of evangelism that is rooted in our history as we embraced the Christian tradition. Our definition of evangelism has historically been rooted in Jesus' proclamation:

> "The Spirit of the LORD is upon Me,
> Because He has anointed Me
> To preach the gospel to the poor;
> He has sent Me to heal the brokenhearted,
> To proclaim liberty to the captives
> And recovery of sight to the blind,
> To set at liberty those who are oppressed." (Luke 4:18 NKJV)

This is a mandate to preach the gospel message or proclaim the Word, to make disciples, and to take seriously our mandate to set people free from the things that oppress them. James O. Stallings put it best when he said that for the African American church, evangelism historically meant "freeing black folks' souls from sin and their bodies from physical, political, and social oppression, and of setting the conditions of existence so that they could achieve full humanity. It was for them a special call from God thrust upon them that was different from that of their white counterparts."[2] The African

American church is unique in that we have always embraced Abraham's and Stallings's definitions of evangelism, which include social change and activism. If your church hopes to reach and effectively evangelize the hip hop generation, the first set of questions has to do with evangelism. I encourage the pastor and the congregation to think about the following questions:

1. How do we define evangelism?
2. How would we define *effective* evangelism?
3. How would we assess the effectiveness of our church in the area of evangelism?
4. How much of our time, energy, and budget is set aside for evangelism? (Remember that everything can't be evangelism, because if evangelism is everything, then it is nothing.)

For a church to be effective in evangelism, the church must be willing to change. But the change that a church makes must be rooted in the Word of God—this Word being both Jesus as the Word and the Bible as the Word. When a church engages in change that leads to the effective evangelization of the hip hop generation, its members will bump into and challenge some church traditions. They will have to ask, What do we change, and what do we protect? They will have to ask, Can we change the practice or the way we do what we have done but maintain the principle or the reason why we do it? In other words, we might accomplish the same end by doing something another way. We may move from a devotion to a period of praise singing, and in the end maybe the same thing is being accomplished.

BIBLE-CENTERED: STANDING ON THE PROMISES

Tradition is loosely defined as customs or practices handed down from the previous generation. In this sense, tradition is good. The church should tell the stories and share its traditions with those of the next generation. Handing traditions down also implies turning them over to the generation that inherits them. Those who hand traditions down aren't to protect the tradition, but rather they are to allow those who inherit it to decide what to do with what they inherited. In the context of the church, is the church protecting tradition? Is the church handing down traditions? Is the church willing to establish new traditions? And finally the church must ask, Is tradition acting as a little god in the church?

Tradition in some churches isn't about what is handed down but rather what is held up, maintained, and defended at all costs. Many of the fights in the local church are about "the way we have always done it." Institutions fight against change and thrive on predictability and stability. Change invites risk and unpredictability, but change is key for a church that wants to grow. Donald Hilliard Jr. says, "One reason many churches fail to grow is because the pastor, the other church leaders, or both, are unwilling to take a risk. Growing churches are risk-taking churches, not in an impetuous or foolhardy way, but in a willingness to try something new, to move in a direction they have never gone before, to step out in faith to pursue a vision even if current circumstances indicate otherwise."[3] Churches that aren't changing, taking risks, and doing new things are stagnant churches that will not grow. And a church that is not growing spiritually and numerically is dying. Some of the African American community's most loyal denominational churches show signs of death and dying. While they hold on to tradition, they are missing an opportunity to influence the lives of the hip hop generation for Christ. Change means that some traditions must be maintained, but many need to be modified, updated, retired, or funeralized. A church that isn't willing to allow traditions to be modified, updated, retired, or graciously laid to rest is a church that is effectively saying, "We want to die."

In his ministry, Jesus was constantly confronted with the traditions of his day. The incident that sticks most prominently in my mind is recorded in the Gospel of Matthew:

> At that time Jesus went through the grainfields on the Sabbath. And His disciples were hungry, and began to pluck

> heads of grain and to eat. And when the Pharisees saw it, they said to Him, "Look, Your disciples are doing what is not lawful to do on the Sabbath!"
>
> But He said to them, "Have you not read what David did when he was hungry, he and those who were with him: how he entered the house of God and ate the showbread which was not lawful for him to eat, nor for those who were with him, but only for the priests? Or have you not read in the law that on the Sabbath the priests in the temple profane the Sabbath, and are blameless? Yet I say to you that in this place there is One greater than the temple. But if you had known what this means, 'I desire mercy and not sacrifice,' you would not have condemned the guiltless. For the Son of Man is Lord even of the Sabbath." (Matthew 12:1-8 NKJV)

The issue here was one of tradition versus need. The Pharisees were more concerned about the tradition than they were about the hungry disciples. The first thing Jesus did was to give them a historical account of what he was doing: picking up the best of the tradition, which was to meet the needs of the people, just as David did. Jesus then made it clear that he, not the Pharisees and their traditions, was the Lord of the Sabbath. Jesus is Lord! The way we have done things in the past are under the same scrutiny as was the showbread or former Jewish customs. In some churches, the tradition has become lord, and even if Jesus came in and tried to change something, he would be stoned. A church that makes its traditions its god is practicing idolatry. God is clear that we are to have no other gods.

Churches have to come to the biblical realization that Jesus Christ is the Lord of the Sabbath and the church. Churches that are willing to challenge tradition must be willing to search God's Word and ask how God's Word speaks to us about what we are to do and what we shouldn't do. The church must also confess that Jesus is the Lord of the Sabbath, and not our church bylaws or *Book of Discipline.* A church that is bound by what men and women wrote as opposed to what God wrote in God's Word is a church that is out of touch with the Spirit of God. If tradition is so rich and deep in a church that the members can't hear a new word from God, they will die a slow death.

To hear from God and to be open to God's Word doesn't mean that everything will change or has to change. God may affirm and confirm what the church is doing, but the church must be open to have a Holy Ghost dialogue with God and God's Word. This isn't a one-time conversation that took place when your particular denomination or congregation was founded. God hasn't stopped speaking. God is always revealing God and God's will to us in an attempt to renew our minds about what God's good, pleasing, and perfect will is for today. Romans 12:1-2 (NKJV) is one of my favorite Scriptures, as it always beckons me to be open to what God is doing new in my life and the life of the church:

> I beseech you therefore, brethren, by the mercies of God, that you present your bodies a living sacrifice, holy, acceptable to God, which is your reasonable service. And do not be conformed to this world, but be transformed by the renewing of your mind, that you may prove what is that good and acceptable and perfect will of God.

Romans 12 does not call us to be conformed to the world, so as we embrace change, we are not to become worldly but to become godly. To become godly may mean that we take what the world has to offer, baptize it in the Holy Spirit, and take it where God can use it. The key to this passage is for the church to be willing to constantly be transformed. Transformation and renewal never stop. The church never arrives at complete revelation but is always asking, What next, God? What kinds of questions should the church be asking about tradition?

1. What are the traditions of our church?
2. When did these traditions start?
3. What is the biblical basis for each of these traditions?

4. Can we maintain these traditions that are biblical in their present form, or do they need to be updated or modified?
5. What traditions are we willing to change? Why or why not?
6. What is the basis of our resistance to changing those things that we aren't willing to change? Is it biblical? Personal? Selfish? Is it because this is the way we have always done it?
7. Are there any traditions in our church that need to be done away with? Why or why not?
8. Are we each willing to support the changing of tradition in our effort to be obedient to God's call on our church to serve this present age? Why or why not?

As the church begins to think about and pray about change, its members are opening themselves up for new vision and revelation. This opening starts when you are willing to challenge the old and change it if necessary. If a church is open to change, it will be receptive of vision. A church that fights change will also fight vision.

VISION: PAST, PRESENT, FUTURE

> Behold, I will do a new thing,
> Now it shall spring forth;
> Shall you not know it? (Isaiah 43:19 NKJV)

God wants to do something new in your church, but the question is, Can you see it? To see what God wants to do in your church requires that the congregation and the pastor be open to transformation or renewal by getting into God's Word and expecting new revelation. It also requires earnest prayer and listening to God constantly (1 Thessalonians 5:17). When churches take God's Word seriously, while praying earnestly, expecting God to do something new, they will receive vision from God.

Vision for local churches needs to be held in tension with the past and present state of the church. Churches have to take into consideration from whence they have come. This is not an exercise that should be anecdotal, but it should be taken literally. It is my prayer that every church has a written history. Every church needs to consider developing some type of archives. As the church considers traditions that are to be handed down, it must clarify the roots of its traditions historically and biblically. As the church looks back, it should help members understand more about their present state of ministry. The present is a product of the past. As the church looks at its past and reflects upon its present, it needs to take a systematic snapshot of what today looks like. This means being honest about your membership. Who shows up for worship and Bible study? Some churches have membership rolls that need to be examined for accuracy. To examine where you are as a congregation will require brutal honesty. To get a current-day picture of the church, the following questions may be helpful:

1. What is our average number of persons attending worship on Sunday morning?
2. What are their age ranges?
3. What percentage of our worshipers are in the age group 1 to 15?
4. What percentage of our worshipers are in the age group 16 to 25?
5. What percentage of our worshipers are in the age group 26 to 35?
6. What percentage of our worshipers are in the age group 36 to 45?
7. What percentage of our worshipers are in the age group 46 to 55?
8. What percentage of our worshipers are in the age group 56 to 65?
9. What is the percentage of our worshipers who are in the age group 66 to 75?
10. What percentage of our worshipers are in the age group 76 and above?

11. How many new members did we take in last year?
12. What were their age ranges?
13. What percentage of those who joined last year are still active this year?
14. If we continue to grow at our present rate, considering our present average age range in worship, what will we look like in ten years?
15. What do we *want* to look like in ten years?
16. What are we willing to change to get the kind of picture we want ten years from now?

Change for tomorrow starts today. The questions above do not complete the list of questions that need to be asked, but rather are only the beginning. Some churches are living in the past, but churches have to deal honestly with what they see on Sunday, not what they claim on the rolls. This calls on denominations, pastors, and laity to be truthful about who is sitting in the pews. This type of honesty will help churches see who they are or are not reaching.

The questions listed above may affirm what you are doing. Let's not assume that it is all bad. In many situations the church is doing a great job. Yet even those churches that are pleased with what God is doing in them right now would do well to continue to ask these questions.

The church must continue an inside/outside approach to ministry: Who is inside the church? Who is outside that we want to get inside? How is God calling us to go outside or reach outside to get those who are outside inside? How is God calling us to change what is inside so that when those who are outside come, we will be relevant and be able to retain them and disciple them into faithful disciples of Jesus Christ? We are moving into talking about vision. What is the vision for the church? Again, Hilliard says, "Every church needs clear vision; otherwise it has no idea where it is going or how it is going to get there."[4] If a church has no vision, it will become lost in the wilderness. Vision serves as a guide or rudder in the change process. As the vision is revealed to the church, it is important that members get on board and support the vision. As the church moves through the process of asking questions and begins to embrace the vision, it is entering a change process. The change process is predictable. Leaders and church members must understand the change process and walk with the church as it goes through its changes.

THE CHANGE PROCESS: A CHANGE IS GOING TO COME

According to *John P. Kotter on What Leaders Really Do,* there are at least eight steps in the change process. I highly recommend this book if you want to deal with each step in depth.[5] Let me at least introduce you to these eight steps and then make some general observations that might get you thinking about what the church has to do if it wants to change.

1. Establish a sense of urgency.
2. Form a powerful guiding coalition.
3. Create vision.
4. Communicate vision.
5. Empower people to act on the vision.
6. Create short-term wins.
7. Produce more change.
8. Institutionalize change.

As the local church looks at its past, present, and future, there should be a sense of urgency. God will speak in this period of examination, and the church must hold on to what it hears. Habakkuk portrays a clear image:

> "Write the vision
> And make it plain on tablets,
> That he may run who reads it." (Habakkuk 2:2 NKJV)

The sense of urgency mustn't come just from the pastor. It is important that the church leaders embrace, support, and share the vision. The vision prospers as church members realize that the vision for their church isn't the pastor's vision, but rather it is God's vision given to the church through the pastor and church leaders. When the church owns the vision as received from God, members will work hard to effectively communicate the vision in such a way that the entire congregation understands and supports the vision. To effectively communicate the vision also means sharing with people practical ways they can get involved in making the vision a reality. To make the vision a reality, it is a given that each member will give a tithe and an offering (Malachi 3:8-12). They must also pray for the vision and actively work to bring the vision into reality. As each member supports the vision, that requires change, by giving tithes and offerings, along with giving time to work in the ministry of the church. Members must also embrace the fact that as they change, even more change will be required.

To move toward realizing the vision is not a one-time act. It isn't voting to approve the vision or sitting in the meeting where the pastor shares the vision and then shouting "Amen!" As the church makes the first moves toward the vision, the initial change will be easier than the changes that will come later. Once the ball of change starts rolling, it will eventually come to the particular part of the church ministry that directly affects you. I am reminded of how my initial embrace of hip hop was easy, but as I embraced hip hop and the hip hop generation, they continued to push me. I felt at times overwhelmed by the push because in the end it wasn't so much about changing the church and how we were doing ministry as much as it became about me changing who I was if I was to be true to the call God had placed on our church and my life. When the change involved me changing how I teach Bible study, the way I preach, the music I listen to, the places I went, and my relinquishing some of my power in the church, yes, I became resistant and fought back. Change isn't easy.

I have found that the older I get, the more difficult change becomes, because I get set in my ways. But my age doesn't excuse me from submitting to God and God's call for the church to serve the present age.

The change process is circular; as change is made and the new way becomes a part of how you do ministry, you will have to start all over again by creating a new sense of urgency for the next wave of change. Change invites new people in. Change calls on the church to do things in a new way. Change calls on the church to open the doors of the church and bring the new people in with all of their stuff, all their different ideas and new ways of thinking.

"THE DOORS OF THE CHURCH ARE OPEN"—ARE THEY REALLY?

How open are your church doors? Are we really interested in new people coming in and making us change even more than we want? At the end of most sermonic presentations in the African American church, the pastor opens the doors of the church. This is an invitation for those who don't have a church home to join or for those who have not confessed Jesus Christ as Lord and Savior to do so. Ironically, the invitation is given while the physical doors of the church are closed. I was always told the doors were closed so that no one could leave! Over my past twenty years in ministry, I have often wondered, as I stood to extend the invitation, just how open are the doors of the church? In our effort to keep people *in* during the invitation, I wonder if that has not also translated into us keeping people *out.* In the church's effort to symbolically keep the world out of the church, we may have locked those in the world out of our world. Don't panic, I am not going to argue that the church become more worldly. What I suggest is that the church ask itself a few more questions:

1. How worldly are we already?
2. Do we wear worldly clothes to church?
3. Do we drive worldly cars to church?
4. Do we wear worldly hair styles to church?
5. Did we graduate from secular universities?
6. Do we put money earned in the world in the offering plates that were made in the world?

7. Do we have worldly alarm systems installed on our church to safeguard our worldly possessions?

Can we be honest and ask how worldly the church is already? The church may be in denial of just how worldly it already is, which leads us to the final point of this chapter when it comes to change and the hip hop generation. When it comes to hip hop, one of the first things I hear is, "We don't want to become too worldly." The passage from the Bible that will serve to push us here is found in 1 Corinthians 9:19-23 (NKJV):

> For though I am free from all men, I have made myself a servant to all, that I might win the more; and to the Jews I became as a Jew, that I might win Jews; to those who are under the law, as under the law, that I might win those who are under the law; to those who are without law, as without law (not being without law toward God, but under law toward Christ), that I might win those who are without law; to the weak I became as weak, that I might win the weak. I have become all things to all men, that I might by all means save some. Now this I do for the gospel's sake, that I may be partaker of it with you.

The question is not, Should the church become more worldly? but How is the church to become more like those it is called to reach? In other words, how is the church to become hip hop in order to reach the hip hop generation? Paul said he became that which he was trying to reach while remaining true to who he was in Christ. I said at the outset of this chapter that I wasn't going to try to dictate to churches what they should do, but I was going to suggest questions the church should be asking. This is one of the central questions the church has to ask and answer as it relates to reaching the hip hop generation: How are we to become hip hop?

In the first chapter of this book we tried to identify the elements of hip hop and define it as a culture. How is the change process of the local church to be culturally driven? What is on the outside that can be brought inside and be fully submitted to God? To be honest with you, I have always struggled with this question. I don't even pretend to know the answer. However, it is a question I have constantly asked myself, as I've had a passion for evangelism from the first day I was called into the ministry.

One theologian has helped me immensely when it comes to the question as to how much of hip hop should be integrated into the church. This theologian is a seminary graduate, pastor, and holy hip hop artist. I am talking about the Ambassador. His compact disc *The Thesis* answers many of my questions.[6] I recommend it to each of you as you, like I, struggle with how to integrate hip hop into the life of the church. Even as I listen to the Ambassador, I leave with more questions, and these questions lead me to more answers, which turn me to new questions. The questions and answers I arrive at serve to push me even more.

I was honest in the introduction of this book as I talked about my struggle with hip hop, rap music, and its inclusion in my life and the church, but my struggle doesn't excuse me from acting. As God continues to grow me and push me, I continue to struggle. I invite you and your church to struggle with me. To believe that we have the final answer means we can't hear a new word from God. This book is an invitation to pray, reflect on God's Word, and ask hard questions as God leads your church to reach the hip hop generation. The church can't run from hip hop; we have to run to it, if for no other reason than to save it.

While the church runs away from hip hop and the world, God has called us to do the exact opposite. When Jesus prayed for the church, he prayed that the Father wouldn't take the church out of the world, but rather that God would keep the church as it went into the world. The church was to be sanctified or made holy not by what it wore or didn't wear but rather by keeping God's word close to their hearts.

> "I do not pray that You should take them out of the world, but that You should keep them from the evil one. They are not of the world, just as I am not of the world. Sanctify them by Your truth. Your word is truth. As You sent Me into the world, I also have sent them into the world." (John 17:15-19 NKJV)

To not be of the world does not mean that we will not take things out of the world and make them submit to the will and ways of God. The African American church has always done that. The church did it with blues music and culture, and now the African American church finds itself back here with hip hop. God is sending the church into the world. A church that goes into the world learns from the world. It understands those who are fully engulfed in the world's system. A church that invites but doesn't go is a church that could easily lose touch with the very ones God has called it to reach. How can the church heal what it won't touch? How can the church touch what it will not look at? How can the church see where it has not gone or isn't willing to go? While the signs on the front of many churches read "All Welcome," the question is, Who doesn't feel welcome when he or she comes into your church? Who leaves because the church service in no way reflects them or their culture? Questions, questions, questions—the questions lead us to new answers and more questions.

GOD, WHAT WOULD YOU HAVE US TO BE?

In the end, the church can't avoid the task of questions and answers if it wants to be true to its calling. It must be willing to go to God and ask, God, what do you want us to be today? This is a daily question, as God will only reveal as much to the church as it can handle. The change process in any church must be under the complete direction of God. God has chosen pastors to lead the church under Jesus Christ, and the change process in any church must be led by pastors who are submitted to God and by parishioners and staff people who are submitted to God and God's pastors. God has not called leaders in the church to fight pastors as they try to follow God. God has called the body together for unity of purpose in vision.

> "I do not pray for these alone, but also for those who will believe in Me through their word; that they all may be one, as You, Father, are in Me, and I in You; that they also may be one in Us, that the world may believe that You sent Me. And the glory which You gave Me I have given them, that they may be one just as We are one: I in them, and You in Me; that they may be made perfect in one, and that the world may know that You have sent Me, and have loved them as You have loved Me." (John 17:20-23 NKJV)

God wants a united church. As each church takes seriously the call to change and reach the hip hop generation, there will be dissension. There will be some in the church who will not understand what the church is doing. The church needs to love these people, but it can't allow them to derail what God is trying to do. The dissenters are not to become gods or to hold up false gods. In some cases, a number of the church's most staunch and senior members will scream the loudest. They will lead the protest, but that doesn't mean it is of God. It may mean that they are not in touch with what God is doing today. They need to be heard and their message prayerfully evaluated. But if they are speaking something different from what God has spoken, to whom will you listen? God said this is God's church: "And I also say to you that you are Peter, and on this rock I will build My church, and the gates of Hades shall not prevail against it" (Matthew 16:18-19 NKJV).

Folk who raise hell cannot be allowed to overthrow God's will of getting people to heaven through his church. People in the church are going to fight hip hop primarily because they don't understand it. The battle with hip hop will be similar to the battle we had with the blues and gospel music, but it is a battle the African American church can't avoid, because too many souls are at sake. Too many of our youth and young adults are living outside of the church, going to jail, being shot and killed, or strung out on drugs. The hip hop nation needs the church, and the church needs the hip hop nation. When the naysayers rise up, the church has to decide who to listen to—God and God's Word or those who chose to speak against God's plan. The choice is yours.

NOTES

1. William J. Abraham, *The Logic of Evangelism* (Grand Rapids, Mich.: Eerdmans, 1989), 13.
2. James O. Stallings, *Telling the Story: Evangelism in Black Churches* (Valley Forge, Pa: Judson Press, 1988), 20.
3. Donald Hilliard, *Church Growth from an African American Perspective* (Valley Forge, Pa: Judson Press, 2006), 22.
4. Ibid., 24.
5. John P. Kotter, *John P. Kotter on What Leaders Really Do* (Boston: Harvard Business School Press, 1999), 92.
6. The Ambassador, *The Thesis,* CD (Cross Movements Records, 2005).

CHAPTER 5
BRING 'EM OUT: EVANGELIZING AND PASTORING THE HIP HOP GENERATION

"I am the good shepherd. The good shepherd gives His life for the sheep. But a hireling, he who is not the shepherd, one who does not own the sheep, sees the wolf coming and leaves the sheep and flees; and the wolf catches the sheep and scatters them. The hireling flees because he is a hireling and does not care about the sheep. I am the good shepherd; and I know My sheep, and am known by My own. As the Father knows Me, even so I know the Father; and I lay down My life for the sheep. And other sheep I have which are not of this fold; them also I must bring, and they will hear My voice; and there will be one flock and one shepherd."

—John 10:11-16 NKJV

The church is called to evangelize the hip hop generation, but the call doesn't stop there. The church is also called to disciple and pastor the hip hop generation. They are our children, and we can't detail this work to the children. Hip hop churches that are made up of all young people aren't healthy families, because healthy families need inter- and cross-generational relationships. The family of God that isn't diverse in age, class, and gender is an unhealthy family. Some suggest that churches who don't feel called to minister to the hip hop generation should partner with other churches that do. But such a partnership abdicates their responsibility to the hip hop generation; African American congregations are called by God to take care of their young. In this chapter we will share with you evangelistic strategies that work. Following this chapter are the stories of four pastors who tell how they succeeded in reaching and pastoring the hip hop generation. Each story is unique, and their stories are not meant to be patterns but rather examples that might inform your ministry. The hip hop generation is waiting on the church to extend the olive branch and invite them back to the church. Here is your chance to improve on what you are doing or to begin your outreach to a generation that is waiting on us.

When it comes to evangelizing the hip hop generation, we know that they are anti-institutions and opposed to institutionalized religion. They see themselves as spiritual but not religious. This is an interesting dichotomy, but George Barna and Robin Sylvan are among those who have been in touch with this population and who have all consistently found this spiritual identity of opposition-to-being-religious.[1] This means that the hip hop generation is looking for spiritual encounters that get them in touch with their feelings, encounters with the holy that are relevant, encounters that are applicable to their circumstances and aren't shrouded in religious language. Much of the language the church uses is a jargon deeply rooted in church culture. Hip hop wants "plain speak" that is direct, honest, and understandable. If you listen to the stories of the four pastors featured in this book, one consistent feature that you find in their work is relevance, clarity, honesty, transparency, and an ability to deal with topics that speak to the now of their congregants' life.

The hip hop generation also wants the freedom to talk back to religious leaders and to God. Hip hoppers are looking for dialogue—not monologues. They have something to say. What they have to say is rooted in their dialogue with God as they struggle in a real world with current issues. They find suspect people who have all the right answers and pretend to have it all together. For hip hop, spirituality is directly linked with getting in touch with themselves and others in meaningful relationships that help them live out their divine purpose. They are more concerned with having a meaningful and enlightened conversation rooted in relationship than with listening to a well-crafted sermon. While sermon preparation is needed and a good sermon is appreciated, they prefer sermons that invite the listener to think and respond with both head and heart. Yesterday's lofty sermons of rhetorical brilliance have little resonance with hip hop. They expect the preacher to have a flow, but his or her flow should be more akin to the structure of rap, in verses and choruses that ring with truth and application instead of flowery language that circles around with big words. This means they want the sermon to be clever, intriguing, twisting, and engaging while staying rooted in story. The crafting of sermons has to be as clever as the best of rap. When you listen to the best rappers, you hear how adeptly they structure it, using a unique play with words to make meaning that moves the listener.

PREACHING TO SAVE HIP HOP

As preachers and teachers seek to be more relevant and be heard by hip hop, a few hints can inform this shift in sermon preparation. According to Kool Mo Dee in *There's a God on the Mic: The True 50 Greatest MCs*, there are some essential components shared by the great emcees or rappers.[2] Ten of the key areas Kool Mo Dee has identified are relevant for preaching to the ears of hip hoppers.

1. *Originality:* Preachers must bring a fresh and creative slant on the text. Hip hop wants to say, "I never thought about it that way before. I heard this preached before but not put like that." For preachers to achieve this goal, they will have to take exegesis of the text very seriously.

2. *Concepts:* Preachers must be able to paint pictures that are multidimensional and present coherent sermons and teaching series that develop an idea from start to finish. Sermon series need to be seen like a compact disc in development and style, one CD consisting of tracks that connect and compliment each other.

3. *Versatility:* Preachers need to be free to experiment with new ways to present the Word, to vary the style and approach they use. This pushes preachers to consider changing or updating their style instead of developing and resting their careers on one style. Hip hop embraces change.

4. *Substance:* One's preaching must have social relevance. Hip hop wants preachers to answer the "so what?" question. Hip hop wants

to see connections as the preacher samples and remixes Scripture with social commentary.

5. *Flow:* Flow is about syncopation and cadence. Preachers with a versatile flow based on the sermon will be heard easier by hip hop. Preachers need to feel free to teach, preach, and teach/preach. Hip hop wants the preacher to "bring it," as the old *skool* would say.

6. *Flavor:* Flavor refers to the preacher's uniqueness in contrast to other preachers. Preachers must bring energy and some sense of fun to their preaching. Hip hop is looking for preachers who have a signature style that engages them, holds them, and brings them close to the preacher and the Word by the power of the preacher's flavor. Remember that hip hoppers like high energy.

7. *Vocal presence:* The voice of the preacher is something else hip hop wants. The preacher should embrace his or her unique vocal qualities. The vocal qualities need to be developed and recognizable. The best of emcees are so recognizable that by the time they finish a sentence or a bar on a track the audience knows just who it is.

8. *Live performance:* Hip hop is looking for a performance. The church may find this suspect, but the best of African American preaching has always been performance. In an entertainment culture, preachers who want to reach hip hop must confront the reality that they are looking for and expecting a great live performance.

9. *Poetic value:* The use of story, metaphor, and simile is also important for hip hop. Preachers who use stories in their preaching to amplify the stories in the Bible and their relevance/application for today's life will resonate with the hip hop ear. They are looking for the tricks and power of the metaphor or the story within the story as a hook to keep them in tune and in touch with the preached and lived word.

10. *Lyrics:* Whether you are a manuscript preacher, no-notes preacher, or freestyle preacher, the hip hop generation is looking for well-developed, well-crafted sermons that flow like lyrics. The preacher who wants to know more about the structure of lyrics should study song structure or the structure of rap lyrics. The power of the lyrics or structure of the sermon is key to hip hoppers; it is how their ears have been trained to hear.

The preacher who wants to reach the hip hop generation and hold them will need to at least consider those ten ideas in sermon preparation and Bible study teaching.

The hip hop generation wants a smart, questioning faith to be developed in their lives. They don't want dogma or heavy doctrine. Teaching churches have done well with young adults because the best of teaching churches encourage their people to think. They empower them to ask questions and analyze the faith with head and heart. Hip hoppers come from a world where they are getting religious instruction and direction—for head and heart—from many of the artists they listen to. The average rapper or neo-soul artist freely offers religious instruction at their concerts and on their compact discs. Many in hip hop firmly believe that they have religious knowledge to some extent and a relationship with God. As preachers preach to them, the preachers have to be sensitive to how they approach the issues of salvation and relationship with God. They must be clear about what it means to be in relationship with God and to be a member of God's church. Yet these topics of salvation and church membership must be broached against the backdrop that many hip hoppers feel they don't need to be "saved" or a member of a local church. To be told that they don't have a saving relationship with Jesus Christ or God insults them. When appeals are made in churches for them to give their lives to Christ, many look at the pulpit with amazement—insulted that someone would think they don't already have such a relationship. They call themselves spiritual but not religious, committed to God but not a church or religion. Evangelistic efforts that understand and appreciate this worldview will do well with the hip hop generation.

BEING IN TOUCH WITH THE HIP HOP WORLDVIEW

For churches and church leaders to understand and be able to communicate with the spiritual worldview of hip hoppers, they have to become conversant with that worldview. I advocate that pastors and church leaders listen in on hip hop culture. We need to frequent the concerts, clubs, coffee houses, smoke shops, record stores, and bookstores; we have to buy their music, listen to their radio stations, and watch MTV, BET, and VH-1. These are the sources that are feeding hip hop its spiritual worldview. I don't know if the church is called to condemn these secular media or transform them, but I feel strongly that we are to understand them and then teach in such a way that we are in dialogue with hip hop. Hip hop needs to know what the real church of Jesus Christ has to offer. They need to know the difference between being spiritual and being a true Christian. They need a real alternative to what they are being offered via hip hop spirituality. I believe the church has the right answer. And I believe that the gospel of Jesus Christ is more than just another alternative. But we must allow hip hop to see this as an option. They have to come to the faith on their own terms. The church needs to be a conduit or causeway where they can feel free to sojourn along their spiritual pilgrimage. Their journey to the faith will not be in a straight line, but if the church walks with them, that journey will end at the foot of the cross of Jesus and lead to a saving relationship with Jesus Christ.

The spiritual journey that hip hoppers follow is one the church must respect and not condemn. They will not come to the faith the way their elders came. They must be allowed to take their unique path to Christ. The church has to realize how much times have changed. When I was a child, you grew up in a church, and when you became of age you were considered a member of your family church. This is not the case for the hip hop generation. Many of them didn't grow up in a church, and they don't have the institutional loyalty of their elders. Therefore the appeal of Big Momma and Granddaddy's church will not do.

The hip hop generation is on a quest to make sense of its own faith and religious decisions. They don't feel that religious or faith-based instruction is the sole property of the church. A recording artist's views on faith are as substantial as a seminary-trained pastor in the eyes of hip hop. That is why it is so important for pastors and teachers in the church to take hip hop seriously. To belittle it—along with its stars and their religious claims—is to belittle the hip hop generation and to say, in part, we are not taking you and your stuff seriously. When the church condemns the rapper who talks about sex on one track and God on the next track, we are missing how hip hop sees the sacred and the secular as being in conversation. It is all part of this messy faith journey, and for hip hop it can't be separated. The church has to respect this as a part of hip hop's spiritual journey and walk with them.

RADICAL, RELEVANT, AND REFLECTIVE OF CHURCH: THE CHURCH HIP HOP IS LOOKING FOR

Churches that will be effective in evangelizing the hip hop generation will be churches that are somewhat radical while at the same time not being too radical. This means that the church's being radical and relevant must be held in tension with the church's bearing some resemblance to the old church. Hip hoppers wants their cake, and they believe they can eat it too. They want the ministry to be cutting-edge by trying new and relevant things that look nonreligious but have a spiritual appeal. These events can be concerts, smokers, coffee hours, luncheons, parties, or practical seminars that are life affirming (not revivals or with God big in the headline); the events have to be designed in a clever way that appeals but doesn't offend. By "clever" we are not implying sneaky or deceptive; we are suggesting that much thought needs to go into planning the event to look like and be something that will touch hip hoppers where they live. They don't want another religious service. They have said no to organized church and yes to events that are more spiritual where they can connect in community.

While the church is doing all of this, we also have to remember that hip hop is not asking the church to be the club. They still want some of those things that resemble the old church. Each church has to walk this fine line of being cutting-edge while being old school. This is a tough walk, but each church must be led by God and its pastor as to how God is calling it to negotiate this balance.

Whatever event a church puts on with and for hip hop must be done with excellence and with hip hop intimately involved in the planning and implementation. Hip hoppers demand high quality ministry that is built with them, not for them. This in part explains why they are attracted to megaministries with professional staff. They want the best while also searching for small, intimate communities. This means that smaller churches can also meet them where they need to be met. Churches who want to reach hip hop have to be as professional as they can—we are talking about polished ministry. It is better for a church to do one thing well that reaches hip hop than ten things poorly.

The quality of the initial experience hip hoppers have with your church will have a lasting impact. Churches shouldn't rush to meet and greet hip hop. Churches need to be prayerful and intentional. Start with what you have. Invite hip hop to the planning table and empower them to build with your church leaders. When we started the Young Adult Ministry at First African Methodist Church in Los Angeles, where I serve on staff, the first thing we did was ask the young adults to sit down with us to plan the ministry with us. This didn't mean that we abdicated our role as leaders, but we engaged in a ministry of mutual submission. As much as I think I know about hip hop, I can always learn. After all, I am a member of the bridge generation; I am not a member of the hip hop generation. I am not going to try and think for them, but I will think with them. Even as you read this book, remember I am sharing what I have learned, but this isn't the end of the story. It is important for each church to get the rest of the story from the hip hoppers in and around the community.

ROUGH BUT CARING: RAW, REAL, AND RELATIONAL

Hip hop is raw, real, and edgy, but its adherents are looking for love. Congregations that aren't loving will not do well with hip hoppers. They have to feel that the congregation—not just the pastor—wants them there and that the congregation is willing to integrate, appropriately, parts of hip hop culture into the life of the church. A soft heart is what they are looking for, but they are not afraid of being confronted with the truth in a real and raw fashion. They want it straight—no chasers—but this must be done in love, not in a way that is demeaning, dogmatic, and "superior." This calls for a delicate balance, but it is one the church must strive to achieve. This means that the church must rethink not so much *what* it says but *how* it says what it says. An honest approach, based on love and sensitivity to the audience, using the language they use, and realizing that hip hop is on a spiritual journey, will go a long way toward reaching the hip hop generation. Once again I point the church back to rap. Listen to how rappers share truth and use story to confront and appeal to the morals and ethics of the audience. While some in the church have dismissed rap music as irrelevant and valueless, in reality there is a value base in hip hop. It is important for the church to hear how value propositions are made in hip hop and consider using this format as a way to share with hip hop the value propositions that are contained in God's Word.

In church culture, what appears to be soft, nice, and understanding is offensive to those who enter the church from the outside. They are either offended by what we say or don't understand what we say. The language of hip hop is a complex language. Learning the language and speech patterns of hip hop can help churches that hope to effectively communicate with them. The key to the communication with hip hop is honesty and transparency. Hip hop will not tolerate folk who aren't "real." By this I mean they embrace struggle, paradox, and tension. Church has a tendency to present things simply or simplistically in dualities of right and wrong. The church has a hard time walking in or dealing with the gray areas. Church culture has a tendency to pretend that those in the church have it all together, especially in our middle-class and upper-class churches. In reality, all in the church are not free from sin, but there is this great Sunday-morning cover up. When churches do talk about sin, it is often limited to sex, smoking, chewing, or drinking—with media culture appearing as the enemy of the church. Sin, the temptation to sin, and falling into sin is a complex topic; it is deeper than many churches are willing to go. Hip hop wants the church to deal honestly with the complexities of sin and the times we all fall into sin. Hip hop does not want the church to sweep all the dirt under the rug. Pull the rug up, uncover the dirt, and help them deal with the complexities and paradoxes that hip hoppers face each and every day. Hip hop isn't afraid to deal with the messiness of trying to live right. This generation understands that many times this reveals an appearance of contradiction, but they are willing to work through this. Their music embraces the appearance of the contradictions, and the church can learn a lot from hip hop in this regard.

KEEPING THE WORLD OUT OR LETTING IT IN: TEACHING THROUGH THE CULTURE

The complexities that hip hop embraces as it relates to sin, holiness, and right living are found in the culture. The greatest teaching about the way hip hop handles these complexities can be found by listening to the average compact disc if you follow it from the first track to the last. There is a flow in the construction of most CDs that can guide the church in both hearing and talking back to hip hop. I've learned to deal with the complexities of hip hop culture by listening, to have success with young adults not by condemning their culture but by embracing their culture. I have found that teaching through the culture gets me where I need to be as it relates to rough, honest caring and growing in my ability to understand their complex minds. The culture educates me and informs me as to what is on their minds. Hip hop culture also lets me know what is at the root of their spiritual quest and what things they want me to walk through as we search together for answers. To get to the point I am describing calls us in the church to respect hip hop culture and realize that the culture has something to teach the church.

Teaching through the culture means using the culture as the church's friend rather than the enemy. The church has to remember that this generation defines itself by a culture it has embraced: *hip hop*. While parts of hip hop culture are unhealthy, other parts of the culture are affirming and life-sustaining. The church can use the culture as a window for dialogue and relationship building while learning from the culture. I am in no way putting the church above hip hop. I am not trying to argue for a hierarchy as much as I am trying to suggest a point of mutual respect and engagement that can inform the church's evangelistic appeal to hip hop. I am not saying that the church should manipulate the culture to trick people into making faith commitments. I firmly believe that hip hop culture has something to offer the church: The church can learn a lot about honesty, truthfulness, and being real from hip hop. I don't want to be misunderstood here. What I am saying is that as the church listens and learns from the culture, these learning and listening moments can be transformed into teaching moments.

Let me offer an example of how I teach through hip hop culture as I understand how hip hop culture sees the church, using my encounter with the recent release from Ice Cube. Ice Cube's latest compact disc, *Laugh Now, Cry Later,* has a cut titled "Go to Church." The chorus of the song has the line, "If you a scared mother ———, go to church."[3] The implication is that only weak or scared brothers go to church. The song raises the issue of what a man is or what it means to be tough and street. If one is street or tough, one doesn't go to church; people handle their business; they do whatever needs to be done to squash battles or beefs with another brother. What I do in my teaching is deal faithfully with this construct of how to resolve disagreements that exist in the inner city. I don't condemn the way to deal with disagreements that Ice Cube and Snoop Dogg present, but I engage it. The fact that war and fights are a part of the Bible is also a reality I bring in this study. I aim to deal intelligently and honestly with the reality that at times a violent response to assault may be biblical. I don't dodge this tension of just war, violence, and pacifism. I don't offer a final answer here, but I point out how the Bible has spoken to this issue in both the Old and New Testaments.

The other allegation Ice Cube makes in this song is that the church hasn't been hard enough or tough enough. I don't dodge this condemnation. I admit the failure of some of our churches in not dealing with maleness. As much as the church is pastor-led, one can argue that it is women-led. The church's tendency to male bash is not uncommon. Jesus has been made weak and not accurately presented as the strong, strapping, young black male that he was. He was a brother who dealt with challenges throughout his ministry. I used the Gospel according to Mark to look at Jesus as a hard brother. This means that I had to work at re-imaging Jesus and the church as hard or tough. This meant taking my students to look at the history of the African American church, which has led all of the major social movements of the African American community. This then took us back to Ice Cube's critique, and we had to ask how we reclaim the tradition of the church being hard and providing leadership again for social change and activism. How does the church reclaim this edge of being on the edge? How do each of us react to Ice Cube, and how can we respond positively by re-imaging the African American church to young African Americans by being what we should be based on what we have been and should be? This is an example of teaching through the culture.

What I have done as a DJ and Bible study teacher is to use the radio play list as my teaching and learning tool. I consciously listen to what the radio is playing, and I look for themes in the top five songs. I then go to iTunes or some other source like Wal-Mart or a record store and buy the music. To break down the lyrics, I go to www.ohhla.com and print the lyrics. I study the song for understanding, not in order to critique. After understanding the song and giving the artist and the art the benefit of the doubt, I allow my teaching to faithfully engage the art, the artist, and his or her work as I put them in dialogue with the Bible. In no way do I belittle or unfairly judge the artist, but I treat them, their work, and their position with the utmost respect. In many instances I don't just deal with the radio song, but I deal with the breadth and scope of the artist's work and his or her own biography. I like to come to the table at study knowing a great deal about the artist and his or her life and work. I may engage the entire album the artist has just released and let it enter into dialogue with the Bible.

The beauty of this approach is that it brings instant relevance and engagement. But more importantly, we are teaching our people how to make their faith inform and engage their daily lives. The principles of fairness are so important when doing this. Bible teachers must take an even-handed approach in teaching through the culture by realizing that many of those who are sitting under your tutelage listen to the culture for direction, affirmation, and religious instruction. To blast the work and put it down does us and them no good. To faithfully engage the work and respect it and find some good or redeeming qualities in it is what will advance your work with the hip hop generation.

REACHING THEM WHERE THEY ARE: BEING IN TUNE AND ON THE INTERNET

The culture tells us where the hip hop generation is. As you listen to the music, read *Vibe* magazine, *The Source* magazine, *XXL* magazine, and tune in to the culture, this will give the church a sociogenerational tracking system to tell you exactly where they are, what they are dealing with, and how to speak to them. The themes are repetitive; the cycle of life that young people are experiencing is in itself predictable. Yet to understand hip hop you can't stop at printed material; you must go to the virtual world of the Internet in which they live.

Hip hop uses the Internet and the virtual world in a complex way to develop community. The construction of their community is linked to the way they share information about each other and the worlds they live in. The explosion of facebook and myspace are just two examples. Churches that hope to effectively evangelize the hip hop generation must think about how to strategically use the Internet—that is, to use the Internet the way the hip hop generation uses it. For hip hop, the Internet is not just about e-mail and visiting web pages; the Internet is about community. It is about being in a space and developing space for communication, relationship building, identity development, values clarification, and a host of other functions. Churches have to catch up with the way hip hop is using the Internet, because this will inform churches on how they can effectively use technology to reach out and touch hip hop. While churches are knocking on doors and street witnessing they could be blogging or podcasting.

The church that wants to reach hip hop will need to rethink how they can use radio, podcasting, and blogging as media to reach hip hop and hip hop squared. Hip hop doesn't tune in to the local religious stations—at least not those who aren't already in the church. Hip hop that lives in the world listens in the world. They are listening to the hottest hip hop station in town, and listening throughout the week. I remember when I was living in Augusta, Georgia, the Rev. Otis Moss III, who contributed a chapter to this book (chapter 9), had a hot radio advertisement on the most popular hip hop radio station in town. It was my teenage daughter who pointed the ad out and told me, "Daddy, you have to hear Rev. Moss's commercial. It is hot." She was listening. Her friends were listening, and when she and her friends decided to visit a church, guess what church they chose? You got it: Rev. Moss's church. The radio is a friend of the church that wants to reach hip hop, and the church needs to think seriously about investing in air time for commercials that use hip hop to reach hip hop. The use of hip hop beats with well-crafted commercials that share with hip hoppers what your ministry offers them will draw attention to your ministry. Ministries must understand that the sign that announces worship times and says "All Are Welcome" is insufficient. The church is going to have to get out there where the young adults and youth are and let them know the church is welcoming hip hop back to church.

The church can learn a lot from the club flyer culture that is hip hop. If you go to any local college campus, club event, or concert, you will get bombarded with club flyers. Club flyers are bold 4 x 6-inch cards printed on glossy cardstock and handed out by people who are unashamedly promoting their events. When you stand in line to go into an event or you're leaving an event, people promoting similar events are handing out flyers. When I have been at these events, concerts, college campuses, or club events, I haven't seen churches promoting their events.

At First African Methodist Episcopal Church in Los Angeles, a major project of our Young Adult Ministry has been to work with a firm to design our website and ministry flyer to look just like a club flyer. We then go to concerts, clubs, and college campuses and hand out our flyers. The response we get is interesting, because the flyer is so well done that the first thing the recipient does is admire the flyer. Thinking that it is a club flyer, a person takes it, and then with surprise says, "Oh, this is a church." The look of amazement is worth all we spent in making the flyer. Normally one of two things happen next: people say thank you or ask questions about what we are doing. They are excited that we are there, not confronting them or street witnessing but only handing out flyers like everyone else in the crowd. We also give away CDs and DVDs of our ministry so they can see and hear what we are teaching and what we are doing.

When we go into the streets to hand out our club flyers, we fit in. We dress hip hop, we talk hip hop, we walk hip hop, and we have all the paraphernalia in terms of flyers and CDs that accompany such an event. People are surprised to see us there when they realize we are from a church. The response is overwhelmingly positive, because where many of the hip hop feel like the church has dissed them, we are reaching out to them. They want the church to reach out to them, welcome them, and show them how the church is integrating hip hop culture into the church. That is why our dress, walk, and talk is so important. We are showing them how First AME Church is becoming hip hop and demonstrating that you can be hip hop and holy. When they see how this is being done, they feel affirmed and are much more likely to visit our website, subscribe to our podcast or videocast, or come to one of our bridge events.

While doing street ministry, if a person pursues conversation with us, we don't invite him or her to worship first. They know church goes on Sunday morning; we aren't doing anything revolutionary by pointing them to Sunday morning. As a matter of fact, we don't invite them to anything that is happening on Sunday morning. The event we want to invite them to may or may not be overtly religious, but it will be something happening relatively soon. We want to give ways to respond to our connection that doesn't lock them in to Sunday. We are trying to get them to give First AME Church and God a second look in the context of Christianity. We may invite them to our Tuesday night Journey Experience, which is a type of Bible study that includes performance, spoken word, and rap. We may invite them to our First AME Church FAME and Faith lecture series, our young adult party nights, a dinner, or other event we have planned with hip hop for hip hop. The key here is making the invitation in a nonthreatening, nonconfrontational way. We leave it open. There is no pressure. If we apply any pressure, it is for them to visit the website. What we have found is that people respond. Once some momentum begins to build around your events and hip hop embraces them, they will spread the word. These events must be on target and done right, though, because if they come and it is not what they expected, hip hop will dismiss you as fast as they will run to you.

The church that wants to reach hip hop needs to think about how to use the regular television and media like U-Tube, videocasting, and streaming video. One thing we know about hip hop is they want what they want when they want it. They are used to pay per view; video on demand; downloading movies, television shows, and videos, and watching them when they want them. In an age of instant access and on-demand, churches will have to explore ways to make their teaching, preaching, and worship services available via the latest technologies. This means not simply keeping up with technology but trying to stay ahead of the curve on how the hip hop generation and hip hop squared is using technology. The scheduling of the television broadcast is not as important as making sure hip hop has unfettered access to the broadcast to record it and play it and replay it at their leisure. This can be done via a pay service, or your ministry may want to offer it for free. I am of the opinion that if a ministry focuses on access to its ministry, the financial rewards will come in other ways.

Hip hop has to know about your ministry in order to be able to support your ministry. If the church is asking them to support the ministry prior to them having access, they may never find out about your ministry. Offering the ministry teaching free of charge via downloads, videocasts, or podcasts is no different from someone turning on the television and watching the ministry for free. The use of technology simply gives hip hop another way to access your ministry in a way that makes sense for them. While its being free can bother some churches—and this is understandable because it costs to do ministry—in the end it will pay off. The church must tap into this cultural phenomena and make ministry teaching and preaching free and easily attainable. Hip hop is not going to fight to find your stuff or steal your stuff, so why not make it accessible and free? If this is seen as a part of evangelism, the church can find a way to budget for it.

Hip hop is looking for a church that has a strong sense of community, is connected to the context in which it serves, has a spirit of excellence, and leads its members in developing a smart faith. As much as hip hop brags about and seeks earthly riches, what they want is relationship. Read Mykel Mitchell's *Word: For Everybody Who Thought Christianity Was for Suckas,* in which Mykel tells his story of living in a world of money, drugs, and sex, but what he really wanted was relationship.[4] It was in Christ that he found himself and a loving Christian community. His life was filled with stuff but lacking love and relationship. He traded in his empty life of materialism for a fulfilling life with Christ.

Mykel's testimony is the story of so many in hip hop. They want more out of life, but they don't know where to find it. The church isn't making it known that we have what they are looking for. They can find what they are looking for by giving their life to God and entering a saving relationship and becoming active members of a local church. I am not proposing they become members of hip hop churches made up only of hip hop. Hip hop needs elders, and elders need hip hop. We have to find ways to show them in love how the church has the answers they are looking for. A church that is warm, loving, and welcoming and that provides a space for hip hop will attract and keep the likes of Mykel. They are looking for Jesus Christ, but they won't find the real deal at the concerts they attend. They will find Jesus in the church, but the church needs to take Jesus to the concert and to the streets; it needs to go and hug the Mykels of the world and open wide the doors of the church via technology, ministry offerings, and integrating hip hop culture into the life of the church.

The four chapters that follow come from four pastors who offer hip hop an excellent ministry with preaching and teaching that speak to head and heart. They are sensitive to the needs of hip hop in their own way. Each has a different approach, but each has worked. Their way is not *the* way but *a* way. We hope that these models will get your church praying about how God is going to use you to reach the hip hop generation. There is no one way to reach them, but there are principles that should inform what a ministry does to reach out to hip hop. This means it is between God and each church how they reach out. It is our prayer that each church, under the leadership of and in submission to their pastors, will take seriously the call to reach out to hip hop.

NOTES

1. George Barna, *Evangelism That Works: How to Reach Changing Generations with the Unchanging Gospel* (Ventura, Calif.: Regal, 1995); Robin Sylvan, *Traces of the Spirit: The Religious Dimensions of Popular Music* (New York: New York University Press, 2002).
2. Kool Mo Dee, *There's a God on the Mic: The True 50 Greatest MCs* (New York: Thunder's Mouth Press, 2003), i.
3. Ice Cube, "Go to Church," *Laugh Now, Cry Later,* CD (Lynch Mob Records, 2006).
4. Mykel Mitchell, *Word: For Everybody Who Thought Christianity Was for Suckas* (New York: New American Library, 2005).

CHAPTER 6
AN ELDER'S PERSPECTIVE: THE HIP HOP PASTOR AS FATHER

JASON A. BARR JR.

Macedonia Baptist Church of Pittsburgh is 103 years old. The senior pastor of Macedonia is fifty-two years old. The membership is intergenerational, and the growth in recent years has been largely among young adults under thirty-five years of age, especially those who have been influenced to one degree or another by hip hop culture.

What accounts for this dynamic has been a question posed to me often over the last six years. I have known there was something different about our ministry, but it is often not until guest ministers, particularly those who visit our church during one of three Sunday morning services, question me about what they see. They have often remarked on how rare it is for a senior pastor as "old as you are" to reach so many young people. It is not that we reach this generation by the thousands that throws many off, because we don't. We reach the hip hop generation by the hundreds. They do, however, make up a disproportionately large share of a worshiping community where the leader is a certified, dyed in the wool, and proud baby boomer. A brief overview of our history may help to set the context of this chapter and explain some of the dynamic at work in our church.

BACKGROUND

Macedonia Church of Pittsburgh was founded in 1903. Its membership for most of its existence has been composed of immigrants from the South, especially Alabama. Macedonia has historically been a working-class congregation with strong middle-class values. Its early pastors were men who often came from the steel mills and coal mines to assume leadership of the church. The last three pastors of Macedonia—the Rev. Dr. William Harvey (also formerly the executive secretary of the Foreign Mission Board of the National Baptist Convention), the Rev. Alfred Pugh (also the former president of the Hampton Ministers Conference), and myself—are well-educated men who in many ways have been different from the profile of the church to which we were called to lead.

What each of us also shares is the fact that we were called to lead a church that was composed of working-class people, with varying degrees of appreciation for education, who embraced middle-class values in relation to socioeconomic success, but also a congregation whose members were older adults. This was very much the picture when I arrived as pastor in 1988. In fact, it was even more so because of the social and economic realities of life in Pittsburgh since the decline of the steel mills and the relocation of the major corporate entities which once called Pittsburgh home to more temperate climates.

I arrived in Pittsburgh and Macedonia in 1988, after a six-year tenure as pastor of a small church in western North Carolina. I was thirty-three years old and grateful for the opportunity to serve God in an urban context. I have always known that I was called to serve the city, in the city. My first few years could be characterized as extreme gratitude for having been delivered from the obscurity and frustration I endured in a small town to the excitement of urban ministry. I was largely oblivious to the relative absence of young people or even the paucity of my own generation in the church.

While I was always committed to evangelism and church growth, it was not until my fifth year as pastor that I became aggressively committed to growing the church and reaching a younger generation. I experienced a profound psychological, emotional, and spiritual crisis and epiphany in 1993. Central to this crisis was the death of an infant son. It was a crucial blow to my wife and me and caused significant changes in my perspective on life. His death, among other significant events in 1993, caused me to rethink church, ministry, and the meaning of life.

It was in 1994 that the worship experiences in Macedonia were expanded and changed. In its early years, Macedonia, like most

Baptist churches prior to 1970, held morning worship and an evening worship experience. Since the early 1970s, Macedonia only offered one morning worship opportunity. In 1994, we began an early worship experience. I started this service with the intent that it would be less structured and more contemporary and would reach the younger generation. Interestingly, the service attracted older people and began to reflect a more traditional, liturgical, and contemplative spirit. It was the later service, the service that I had decided that would probably remain the same, that became more celebrative and contemporary.

This was the beginning of the introduction of large numbers of younger people into our worshiping community. What must be noted, however, is that the younger generation that was attracted to our church in this time period was not, by and large, postmoderns or young people who had been influenced to a large degree by hip hop culture. From 1995 until around 2000, Macedonia attracted young adults and young adult families (under thirty-five years of age) who had grown up in church and who were educated, middle class, and upwardly mobile. Their attire did not differ significantly from that of the older church members. They were not as given to following traditional dress codes for worship, but neither did their attire reflect the trends among those influenced by hip hop culture.

I was very comfortable with this group. They were, after all, "my kind of people." I was intentional in my efforts to woo and win them into our fold. Not only were we attracting the baby busters, but we were also attracting large numbers of baby boomers (my generation). All of us were coexisting rather well. The struggle was with the older generation (the builders). Their struggle was, in my estimation, rooted in their loss of influence over and control of the dominant culture within the life of the congregation.

We experienced explosive growth in this period. In a three-year period, our worship attendance increased from 375 worshipers per Sunday to over 1,000 worshipers per Sunday. All of this was occurring in a city that had lost one-half of its population in the forty years prior to our growth. This was also a community whose population had declined from a high of just under 50,000 residents in 1950 to below 10,000 residents in 2000. The city of Pittsburgh was getting smaller; the community in which Macedonia was located (the Hill District) was getting smaller. Macedonia, however, was growing by leaps and bounds.

Our church was growing so fast that by 2000 we were forced to begin a third Sunday morning worship opportunity. In hindsight, we probably waited two years too long to do this. It had become common for people to be turned away and for us to place chairs in the aisles to accommodate those who were able to get access to our sanctuary. Macedonia sits in the heart of a residential community. Consequently, the police and residents were becoming increasingly frustrated by the traffic jams created by our activities.

We had been worshiping at 8:00 and 10:45 a.m. each Sunday. It was the 10:45 service that created the most problems for us. When we went to a third service, we decided to worship at 7:45, 9:45, and 11:45 a.m. It was our initial thinking that the old early-service crowd would shift to the 7:45 service, and that the old 10:45 crowd would split between the new 9:45 and 11:45 services. Not so. What happened created a shift in the life of our congregation that affected us in many ways, but none so apparent as how it affected who we reached.

Many of the people who attended the old 8 a.m. service began coming to the new 9:45 a.m. service. This was especially true of young families who believed that 9:45 was more family friendly than the old 10:45 service or the new 7:45 service (the fifteen minutes were quite important to them). The larger surprise was that overwhelmingly most of the people who attended the old 10:45 service shifted to the new 9:45 service. The end result was that our new 9:45 service was almost as crowded as the old 10:45 service. There were also fewer people in the early service, yet still more than enough to justify its continuance.

HERE THEY COME

What emerged in the new 11:45 service, the late service, and for all practical purposes, the new service, surprised me and continues to baffle me. In March 2000, a new element emerged in our worshiping community that I either did not know was there or that found a way to our church because of this new time of worship. It was clear from age, behavior, appearance, disposition, response or the lack thereof, and even level of commitment, that an entirely different type of person was becoming attracted to our church. I was not altogether familiar with all of the implications of the term "hip hoppers" at this time. In retrospect, we were experiencing the presence of a new generation of churchgoers known as the hip hop generation. They were coming and joining in large numbers.

It was clear to me, especially at the new late-morning service, that something different was happening in our church. I was not always comfortable with it either. While there were adults much younger than I present at the other services, especially the middle service, it was clear that a different type of people was present at the new late service.

They often came very late, walked quite frequently during the service and sermon, talked when they were not supposed to, said things that were inappropriate given the setting, but also were quiet at points when there would be joyful celebrations in the other services. It was clear to me that I was failing them as a preacher. I never felt that I connected with them as I had done with those who attended the earlier services. I was frustrated week in and week out. I often expressed my frustration to them. They would simply look at me with confusion and what I perceived to be frustration. What intrigued me more than anything, however, was that they kept coming back. Not only did they keep coming back, but they kept joining.

Even up to this present day, and more so in 2005 and 2006 than ever, the largest number of people who join our church are people under thirty-five years of age, and especially those who attend this late service. These are people who almost never get dressed up to go to church, guys who wear their pants below their buttocks, females with multicolored hair and styles akin to those seen on videos. These are people who did not grow up in church, and they have little or no familiarity with the Bible. They have been or remain users and abusers of drugs, and they have and continue to experiment with all forms of sexuality. The new element that is part of our worshiping community is not religious but often very spiritual. They do not embrace or even understand the forms and rituals associated with the faith tradition to which they are united, but they are on a serious quest to know and experience God and the spiritual life. They are very suspect of the institutional church and its authority figures, but they appear to be drawn to the personality behind the authority.

What has drawn these young people whose lives and backgrounds are so different from the senior pastor, and indeed the lay leaders, to our church in such disproportionately large numbers?

WHY DO THEY COME?

I have been asked this often. I have been asked by outsiders who are often amazed, and by insiders who are often irritated (at least in the early years). My answer is usually, "I don't know." I really don't. In recent years I have been forced to wrestle with the question. I have been invited to do workshops, retreats, and seminars across the country on developing a multigenerational church or on how to reach the hip hop generation from the perspective of an older senior pastor. It is that wrestling that has helped me to offer some possible and plausible answers. Even then, I must still caution that my most honest answer to the question of why they come to our church is *I don't know.*

I would also like to add the caveat that what I offer here is not a "how to" or "this is the way" approach to reaching the hip hop generation. There are others who do this much more intentionally than I ever would, and those whose approaches and styles of ministry are vastly different yet who are equally and even more successful. The following is simply the gleanings that are the result of my experience.

First, I have to admit that I have always had a passion for young people and people younger than I. I do not understand what the source of this passion is. I do know that it has always been there. I was never a youth pastor, at least not in title, nor have I ever been asked to preach a lot of youth services or youth revivals, even when I was a young preacher. But I have always had a passion for young people. I have always had a desire to see young people be and become all that God intended for them. I have always been attracted to young people who made mistakes or who were born and nurtured in adverse circumstances overcoming the odds and becoming a success.

This passion served me well in my first pastorate in western North Carolina. It was often the source of pain in my early years at Macedonia. Now, as a pastor with twenty-five years of experience, I have led the church to openly declare that we are a church that "majors in minors." Although the young adults who are attracted to our church are not now minors, they are an extension of my passion for those younger people who were not introduced to Christ or life in the Spirit at an early age. I am passionate about seeing the hip hop generation become a joyous and volitional congregation who declare that "every knee should bow, of things in heaven, and things in earth, and things under the earth; and that every tongue confess that Jesus Christ is Lord to the glory of God the Father" (Philippians 2:10-11 KJV).

Second, I have come to understand that many young people are attracted to my transparency. I do admit that I tend to be very transparent in the pulpit. I hope I do this without being a spiritual exhibitionist. I am very honest about my struggle with life, with living consistently with the expectations of the faith, and my frailty. While I do not always share all the details regarding my humanity, I share enough of them that it is clear to others that I consider myself a "project in process."

My transparency is a result of my reaction to the hypocrisy that I struggled with as I grew up in the church. My early years in Christianity were nurtured and shaped by an evangelical and fundamentalist perspective on the faith. From my perspective, those who accepted Christ were "new creatures" who had been changed but who rarely admitted how much they struggled with being everything they declared they had become. My response has been to admit that God has changed me, God is changing me, and there are some things that I struggle with, and struggle with intensely.

I only came to understand the attraction of this aspect of my personality some years ago. Many of the young adults in the church, both those who had and had not been influenced by hip hop culture, began referring to me as "Pastor Keep It Real." I came to understand that this was a positive for them. I also understood that this aspect of my personality had often been a turn-off to many of the older generation of Christians I had led, and often many of my own generation.

The third thing that I believe attracts the hip hop generation to our church is the fact that our church accepts all people without being judgmental. Are there judgmental people in Macedonia? Yes. There are some very judgmental people in our church. But, for the most part, the culture is very accepting of differences. That is so, I believe, in part because its leader tends to be nonjudgmental. This is not to say that I do not believe that we have a standard to uphold. I believe that we must hold up the standards of holiness as espoused in Scripture. My preaching and teaching do not compromise those standards. But I also see a generation of people who often have never been made aware of the standards and who are in need of a word of grace. It is my contention that far too often the church gets so hung up on the fault and rarely sees the need.

As I have come to know many of these young people over the years, and indeed as I have come to understand people in my experience as a minister, I have learned that it is difficult to correct a fault in a healthy way unless you see and speak to the underlying need. I believe that my preaching and teaching ministry embodies that approach. This has been true ever since I started preaching in 1980. What I have come to understand is that it speaks to a deep need among many young people today whose lives and values have been shaped by forces that are antithetical to the message of Christ and the Christian church.

The fourth element that I think is important in reaching the hip hop generation is understanding their culture while remaining true to who I am. Over the years I have become intentional about understanding hip hop culture. I will occasionally speak the language, but never to the point where it defies the fact that I am over fifty years of age. I speak the language to connect to the culture, but never to become one with the culture. I have also sought to understand why the culture's worldview is as it is, while also constructively correcting it when it contradicts what I believe is the core of the Christian gospel.

One of the things that has helped me in this regard is being a father of a teenager. For years I said I could not understand rap. Interestingly, as my son moved toward adolescence and it was obvious he was listening to this art form, it became important for me to understand it. Now, not only do I understand the words (sometimes to my stunned amazement and chagrin), but I am also coming to understand what shapes the culture and can speak to it intelligently and not just reactively.

The fifth thing that has become clear to me regarding the hip hop generation is their need for healthy father figures. Many of them have not been fathered and do not have any understanding of a stable father in their lives. This is where the elder's perspective I bring to this book is perhaps most unique. I am old enough to be a father to most of those who have been shaped by hip hop culture. It has become amazing to me how many of them look to me as a father. It has been amazing how with each passing Father's Day, how many Father's Day cards and gifts I receive from young people for whom I am not their biological father.

Finally, the hip hop generation makes up a large part of the staff of Macedonia Church of Pittsburgh. The worship pastor, new member-s' pastor, youth pastor, caring and visitation pastor, communal life pastor, office administrator, and pastor's executive assistant are all under thirty-five years of age and have been influenced by hip hop culture, to varying degrees. It has been said that "what you place before the people, you will see in the pew." If this is true, it explains why we attract as many young people as we do.

I will admit that this is also a challenge for a senior pastor over fifty. It is a challenge because the younger generation, and especially those shaped by hip hop culture, have been shaped by a very different set of values regarding morality, work ethic, professionalism, respect for authority and boundaries. I constantly find myself challenging them on their norms and either asserting what I believe to be the norms in fact or wrestling with the fact that different does not always mean deficient. Whatever the case, it is not always easy.

CHALLENGES

There are some challenges regarding reaching the hip hop generation when the senior pastor is an elder. I readily own that we have little to no difficulty in reaching this community. We do struggle with developing consistency with them, getting them discipled, and getting them connected to the larger culture of the church.

I have observed an interesting phenomenon in this regard. Once many in this generation do become discipled and get connected, they often cease attending the late service consistently and instead attend one of the two earlier services. This has led one of my colleagues to remark, based on this observation, that our late service is a seeker service, albeit an unintentional one. This observation has caused me to not be as frustrated as I once was regarding the struggles I initially had with this crowd. It does, however, remain a challenge.

I am most grateful for the fact that Macedonia is answering the challenge related to whether we have a future. We are reaching a generation and equipping them to ensure that our witness will continue for years to come. I have witnessed many churches where I question whether they will be viable entities in the next fifty years. Because of the grace and goodness of God, I am proud to say that Macedonia is not one of them.

CHAPTER 7

HOLLA IF YA HEAR ME: THE HIP HOP PASTOR AS PEER

JAMAL-HARRISON BRYANT

In more than thirty universities within and outside the United States, the language of hip hop culture has been established as a course that examines the hip hop cultural movement. Such universities include Stanford University, Harvard University, University of Massachusetts, UCLA, Berkeley, University of Pennsylvania, and various universities in France, Germany, South Africa, England, and other nations. "Hip hop" has become a cliché in academic spheres, galvanizing fields as diverse as linguistics, English, religious studies, anthropology, and philosophy. It amazes one to discover that a young generation of scholars who grew up rapping (MCing), DJing (audio mixing and scratching), break dancing, and tagging (graffiti) is proudly bringing the culture of the street into the classroom. Language has become the primary tool with which one can gain a thorough understanding of the culture.

In interpreting the culture, one needs the revelation of hip hop as a language used to communicate ideas to a group of people who understand it. In 1998, an American Anthropological Association meeting agreed that burgeoning hip hop communities existed in Japan, Europe, South Africa, and South America. Now, more than thirty-five years after hip hop got its start in the black urban scene of the 1970s, this complex, riveting mixture of sound, rhythm, dress, attitude, and poetics has become a universal culture. You can't go to any youth culture event in any capital city on the globe and not find youth talking about a unification through break dancers, graffiti artists, rappers, and DJs (the four groups within the hip hop culture). In his trip to

Tokyo, my friend Ronnie recounts that he saw five teenagers with 50-Cent tee shirts and caps on—the teenagers could barely speak English, but they were fluent in street slang.

The church needs to recognize that hip hop is a language to be used as a vehicle to reach a generation who can't hear what the church is currently saying.

> If the church uses hip hop with a level of integrity as a bridge to take the gospel to a group of people who can't understand gospel music or church lingo, then we shall have evangelized using the language *they speak*. Unfortunately, the church is misguidedly making ministries who aren't prepared to minister to young people and believe that if they use hip hop, young people will join them. As a result, we are witnessing ministries unsuccessfully using hip hop to try to appeal to people who they aren't prepared for. If you are a minister called to suburban ministry, don't try to do urban ministry. Find someone who has that call and pull them into your ministry.[1]

"To thine own self be true," wrote William Shakespeare. In other words, you have to find who you are. You cannot become who you are not. People from the streets have an acute sense of discernment as to whether you are artificial or sincere. One of the things I learned from the book by Martin Luther King Jr., *Principles of Leadership*, is to surround myself with my deficit. Have people around you with qualities that are missing in your life.

Everybody doesn't have a call to this culture and age. If you are uncomfortable listening to their music to address their concerns, or being in their environment to positively influence them, then you have to understand that you haven't been assigned to them. Although everybody doesn't have a call to them, everybody can be welcoming to this generation. Within our worshiping experience, we use the spoken word, dance, and visual arts to present biblical truth. We've used hip hop culture through fashion to create a "dress-down" during summer seasons.

People don't feel less important in our church if they don't come wearing their best. Most young churches that have been labeled hip hop churches have the integrity and grace to reach the hip hop generation.

The biggest percentage of my church is between the ages of eighteen and thirty-five. From its conception, my vision was to establish a church that is not churchy, and I needed the street to become that church. I purposed to target people who have little or no church background or who view the church as irrelevant (the unchurched). Ever since it came into existence in the Bronx in the 1970s, hip hop has been about inner-city and lower-class life. This culture challenges us to revisit how we present the truth of the gospel to young people today. Consequently, modern preachers should return to the drawing board and to discussions on the approaches Jesus used in dealing with the poor and the outcasts of his day. To understand the culture of the modern teenager, one needs to evaluate hip hop as a culture and not just a symbol of music. It's not just about a style of music—but a lifestyle.

In *Hip Hop America,* Nelson George records:

> Now we know that rap music, and hip hop style as a whole, has utterly broken through from its ghetto roots to assert a lasting influence on American clothing, magazine publishing, television, language, sexuality, and social policy as well as its obvious presence in records and movies.... [A]dvertisers, magazines, MTV, fashion companies, beer and soft drink manufacturers, and multimedia conglomerates like Time-Warner have embraced hip hop as a way to reach not just black young people, but all young people.[2]

Before I founded Empowerment Temple, I embodied myself in the culture of the street, so that the street would be acclimated to the church and the church would be welcoming to the street. I did my own anthropological study to find out the things that would repel the street from the church and what the church needed to do to attract people from the street. One of the things I noted was that people at the street level had disdain for pastors because pastors were up on a pedestal. I noted that I had to take the time to openly share my story.

The key to effectively connecting with the hip hop generation is to understand their values and "keep it real." The hip hop culture's passion for honesty must spill over into the congregations who want to reach out to this diverse generation. We are all on a journey, and we have to model that journey. If I give the illusion of having it all together, then I take away the need to lean completely on Jesus. This generation is searching for leaders who will shatter the "title crap" with just being themselves, available, and address issues and not images the generation is facing. You have to model what you want others to do. If you want people to be transparent with their struggles and to pursue growth, then that is the very thing you must model to them. If you want people to genuinely love Jesus, then, as a leader, you must model real love for Jesus.

Failing the eleventh grade, having a child out of wedlock, failing my own singlehood while being saved and being transparent with it, my own journey was a symbol of being honest about my love and desperate need for a Savior and an invitation for others to join me in the journey. I obtained a GED certificate and went on to further my education, graduating from Morehouse College, Duke University, and Oxford University in Great Britain. When I fathered a child out of wedlock, optimism did not seem to help what looked like a limited and diminished future. One thing plagued me—I could not settle for anything short of supernatural success. Failure was not an option, and mediocrity was not a choice. With a child depending on me, I realized that every choice, from then on, would not affect just me but also my seed (inheritance). I therefore chose my way into a better life.

In starting the church, I took the time to lay out a forum on how I could draw in those who were anti-church but who were pro-kingdom. It is said that more than half (54%) of unchurched adults consider themselves to be Christian. When David was raising up his troops, he brought together people who were disfranchised, broke, or misaligned. "David left Gath and escaped to the cave of Adullam.

When his brothers and his father's household heard about it, they went down to him there. All those who were in distress or in debt or discontented gathered around him, and he became their leader. About four hundred men were with him" (1 Samuel 22:1-2 NIV). David was the kind of person who God referred to as a person with God's own heart: "the LORD has sought out a man after his own heart and appointed him leader of his people" (1 Samuel 13:14 NIV). I therefore determined to go after the heart of God and the hearts of people, simultaneously.

In November 1999, I summoned fourteen friends to my home. Upon meeting in my living room, I began to share my *empowering vision* of a church addressing the spiritual needs and concerns of young adults ages eighteen through thirty-five and having them in leadership positions. The church would focus on empowering believers spiritually, developing them educationally, exposing them culturally, activating them politically, and strengthening them economically, through which they would receive power. As the members become empowered, they would empower the broader community, making it the new church for a new generation—not bound by traditional, denominational procedures.

Monday night planning meetings with prayer, Bible study, and tithes moved from my home to the Baltimore Grand, located downtown at 401 West Fayette Street. The small planning team became an organization under the name of Exodus, with five officers, trustees, ambassadors, media, and a temporary facility. The Facilities Committee transformed the Baltimore Grand from a nightclub/banquet hall into a sanctuary. The church changed its name from Exodus to the Empowerment Temple. Bishop Vinton Anderson, the former presiding bishop for the Second Episcopal District, was petitioned to admit the church into the African Methodist Episcopal Church, and thus it became the Empowerment Temple African Methodist Episcopal (AME) Church.

It should be noted that I began the church with my ten thousand dollars in savings, which I used for marketing the church, spreading fliers at shopping malls, placing billboards on buses, and ads in newspapers and radio stations. Fliers and postcards were distributed in nightclubs and at secular concerts throughout the greater metropolitan Baltimore area. We had what was called a Street Team that would target any social event, people coming out of the Lyric, the Meyerhoff. We mainly target people from eighteen to thirty-five. Be it hip hop concerts or clubs, the Street Team was out there when people were coming out on Saturday nights, inviting them to come to church on Sunday. Churchwide marketing included tee shirts, buttons, license plate holders, and car flags. A website was established, and my broadcast, *Keeping It Real,* aired Sundays on WEAA 88.9 FM.

By the end of January 2000, a core group of forty-three had joined, and the church was incorporated on March 20, 2000. In the early stages, the ministry drew modest numbers. Then, nine months into the launch, I preached a sermon that would be the watershed for the ministry. It was titled "Foreplay: Sexual Healing for Spiritual Wholeness" (it's now a bestseller). I examined how the church preaches abstinence yet doesn't openly discuss sex. I therefore needed a nontraditional method of approach. The congregation grew, prompting the need for more than one service and bigger venues—first, Coppin State University and then Walbrook High School. By this time, we were a cutting-edge, hip-hop, urban, inner-city, and gospel-outreach church committed to ministering to the hip hop culture at their point of need.

On Resurrection Sunday, April 23, 2000, The Empowerment Temple held its inaugural service at the Baltimore Grand. The sanctuary and the overflow room were filled with more than thirteen hundred people, and more than one hundred people accepted the invitation to discipleship. During the Baltimore Grand period, April 2000 to August 2000, the Steward Board responsible for the spiritual leadership, guidance, and baptisms, and the Lay Organization responsible for organizing and training the laity of the AME Church were added. In addition, the ministries included music, public relations, and the Adam Clayton Powell Political Action Committee. The church held two Sunday services—Leadership Summit at 8 a.m. and Survivors Service at 9:30 a.m. Ten percent of the offerings were tithed or sowed into local, national, and international nonprofit organizations. The weekly services included Empowerment Hour Service, Survival Seminar, Bible Study/P.H.A.T (Prayer, Healing, and Teaching) on Tuesday, and workout (evangelical outreach) on Wednesdays.

Due to the Downtown Revitalization Initiative, the congregation moved from the Baltimore Grand to the James Weldon Johnson Auditorium on the campus of Coppin State College, now Coppin University, in August 2000. In four months, the church grew to more than 1,200 members. By November 21, 2001, the membership has exceeded 4,000, outgrowing the premises at Coppin University. In 2002, the church was moved to Walbrook Senior High School at 2000 Edgewood Street. By this time, I was more than determined to build a sanctuary that would be located in Baltimore, near public transportation, and not anywhere near other AME churches. By the grace of God, on February 15, 2004 (The Year of Open Doors), we triumphantly marched into our 2,500-seat sanctuary located at 4217-21 Primrose Avenue.

Today, the Temple empowers believers *spiritually* via live broadcast of three Sunday services and Tuesday Bible studies through Internet streaming, men's/women's Bible studies on Saturdays, and Teen Temple on Sundays. With a mission to "Empower the World through the Word," the *Power for Life* broadcast is heard weekly across the United States, in the Caribbean, in England, and throughout the continent of Africa. To empower believers through *education,* the church opened the Empowerment Academy, an elementary school for children in pre-K through second grade. To empower the *community,* the Empowerment Temple Family Life Center Learning Institute was opened. *Culturally,* the church empowers lives through the Drama Ministry, Dance Ministry, Music Ministry & Creative Arts, and the Spoken Word (Poetry) Ministry. The Empowerment Economic Coalition Inc. (EEC) spearheads the *economic* empowerment programs in the church and community. *Politically,* the church has registered more voters than any other church in Baltimore. The church has earned the distinction of being the fastest-growing AME church in the world. The backbone of my advertising has been on a street level: on R & B stations, secular markets, and nightclubs where I can find the people that I am interested in. I don't want to recycle other churches' people.

Many churches miss the mark when they try to do a hip hop packaging but don't have a hip hop presence. My church doesn't have a whole lot of rap music going on, and we don't have people doing break dancing across the screen, but my church is labeled a hip hop church because I embody the hip hop persona. When you look at the hip hop moguls like Jay-Z or Puffy, they are not running around in straight suits, but they now have on suits. Unfortunately, churches that are trying to reach this culture are now putting on straight suits, not realizing that the culture has changed. These hip hop gurus are more than just rappers; they have taken the hustle of the street and turned it into a Wall Street economy with clothing lines.

One of my mandates is to make sure that I meet the culture where they are but not keep them there. The same way they come in the door is not the same way they leave. As many churches wrestle with embracing hip hop, an increasing number of hip hop congregations are emerging, a trend that is going to transform the urban church. Modern churches should be designed to permeate every facet of a parishioner's life, offering health and wellness programs, restaurants, credit unions, private schools, and daycare centers. "What you get is a religion that works," according to Howard University associate professor Harold Dean Trulear. "Some people call it a 'psychologized' version of faith. It's almost like group therapy; they really focus on helping people cope with life's problems and issues."[3]

Though hip hop has achieved a secure place in popular culture, its colorful styles come with a dark, disturbing element. The very success of this genre has created something of a schism in hip hop culture. For many parents and leaders, much of today's most popular rap/hip hop music sets off moral alarms. However, everyone who uses English as a language doesn't use it to empower. This doesn't stop the church from using English as a language. For instance, there are numerous movies and musical recordings that aren't hip hop but are violent, sexual, and perverse. Many people spend most of their time focusing on the negative, without realizing that the language can effectively be used to minister to the people who are using it in a wrong way. According to Russell Simmons, hip hop's first millionaire entrepreneur, one reason hip hop is so popular is because of the resistance it has met. The more resistance there is—and the more controversy there is—the more people are going to want to buy it.

I embrace the hip hop cons (negatives) to make them pros (positives). For example, one of the cons is the materialism that hip hop culture tries to embrace: get the Benz, the cars, the gold, similar to what prosperity ministry has. The difference is that the culture doesn't tell them how to do it in a work ethic, nor do they teach the principle of sowing and reaping. I stress being empowered for success, and what I don't convey in words, I do with imagery—much of which is rooted in hip hop. Here I am driving a frosty green 2006 Bentley. The church ought to be the place where we encourage people to get everything without making stuff their priority.

In the words of Efrem Smith, "When one sees hip-hop as more than just rap music, as a whole culture, new doors open for evangelism, and we can become learners, observers and missionaries to those living in hip-hop culture and those influenced by it. In our contemporary urban culture, we can be like Paul when he addressed the altars built to unknown gods in Athens and used them as vehicles to present the true God who can be known intimately through Christ Jesus."[4]

NOTES

1. Jeff Johnson, conversation with author, during *Cousin Jeff Chat,* Empowerment Temple, Baltimore, MD, 27 August 2006.
2. Nelson George, *Hip Hop America* (New York: Penguin, 2005), ix.
3. Harold Dean Trulear, quoted in Joe Burris, "Feeling Empowered," *UniSun,* August 6, 2006, available at http://www.baltimoresun.com/unison.
4. Efrem Smith and Philip Jackson, *The Hip-Hop Church: Connecting with the Movement Shaping Our Culture* (Downers Grove, Ill: InterVarsity Press, 2006), 47.

CHAPTER 8

BAD BOY FOR LIFE FROM PUFFY TO DIDDY: THE HIP HOP PASTOR AS COUNTERCULTURAL MODEL PROFESSIONAL

WILLIAM H. CURTIS

There are many ways to access and reach the hip hop generation. One of the reasons I was asked to contribute along with the others in this volume is that at Mount Ararat we have done so in a way that is unique. I am not a hip hop preacher, and I don't include references to hip hop culture in my messages. I have found that many of those of the hip hop generation who come to Mount Ararat—aka "the Mount"—come for a fresh word that challenges hip hop. They come for a respite from what they hear every day in hip hop culture. My approach to reaching the hip hop generation is contextual and true to who I am. I am a seminary-trained preacher who loves to exegete Scripture and speak to both head and heart. Preaching quality messages that are contextually relevant is what is most important to me and my ministry. As each pastor and congregation seek to reach hip hop, I point out the one thing I have learned and stress: Be true to your local context. As much as you can learn from reading books such as this one, you must take what others have learned, pray over it, and ask the big question: How can this work in my context? Or what would this look like in my context?

Your personal history and the history of your congregation are as important as is being in touch with hip hop culture. A sense of the history of your city is important, because it will inform how you reach out, as it did with us at the Mount. Mount Ararat is located in Pittsburgh, Pennsylvania, the steel city that has gone through a stage of rust, drought, and dwindling population. The city has endured the downturn of the steel industry by recreating itself into a new type of urban city. The rebound of Pittsburgh has been linked to an attempt to diversify its economy and build on the anchors that remained in the city after the end of its steel industry age. The city has become a medical center along with having several colleges and universities preparing young people for lives of productivity and social contribution. African Americans who once relied on the steel industry as a major source of employment have now moved into the economic center of Pittsburgh. For young adults, professional life in the inner city came to be in the new service economy in which banking, insurance, retail, and tourism, along with the medical and education professions, have become key inroads. The socioeconomic reality of Pittsburgh and our being in touch with this shift served to fuel the growth of the Mount. These young African American professionals became our members.

THE MOUNT PRESENT TENSE

Every weekend the Mount holds four services. In those four services we minister to approximately six thousand out of the more than nine thousand who claim membership. Three out of the four services each weekend will be attended predominantly by young adults who make up more than two-thirds of the church's overall population. I have been asked repeatedly about the church's ability to attract so many young adults, including those heavily immersed in the hip hop culture that dominates this age. The question of why they come and stay may surprise many of you. It may surprise you because the Mount has taken a countercultural approach in some ways. We have not so much embraced hip hop culture as the hip hop generation has embraced us. While many have tried to become hip hop, we have tried to engage hip hop by presenting sound biblical preaching and teaching in the context of a powerful, well-designed worship experience. The hip hop generation is not a monolithic group. Hip hop is diverse, and one thing they love is quality options. The Mount provides a quality option for them that is not steeped in hip hop culture per se but rather speaks to hip hop culture with a love and sincerity that appeals to them, awakens them, and confronts them.

We found that hip hop is not afraid to be confronted and empowered by biblical truth. They like to be challenged. The young professionals and working-class African Americans who come to the Mount don't come because I am quoting the latest rapper; they come because they want to hear the truth. They want me to preach straight to them and not belittle them by trying to be something that I am not. The approach that we have taken at the Mount to reach this eclectic generation is rooted in our unique qualities as a church and my qualities as a pastor. In the end, we are going to suggest that every church that wants to reach hip hop not mimic us or any other church, but rather understand its unique qualities and personality as a pastor and congregation and then build on them as a means of outreach. At the Mount, we identified what was unique about us and then built on those unique traits. As we made them an amplified part of our ministry, we began to see how these, along with the context in which we served, would help us reach young adults, commonly referred to as the hip hop generation.

The Mount's unique qualities fall into the three broad categories. The one uniqueness is who I am as a pastor and preacher/teacher. Second, we took into consideration the city we served in. As stated earlier, Pittsburgh was going through transition, and this made it a mission field where people needed a place as a social and religious outlet. Third, we understood the unique position of the Mount as a church. Our church's history and position in the city as one of the most attractive havens for professionals was a reputation and foundation that we embraced and built upon as well.

BACK TO THE BEGINNING: A CALL TO THE MOUNT

In 1997, I was called to Mount Ararat following an emotional split with the previous pastor, whose gifts and charisma were awe-inspiring. Many families found themselves having to choose between following the pastor, who founded a new church not far from where the

Mount is located, or staying at the Mount with the population remaining being older and more traditional. This feeds into our unique identity. We had a core of more mature members upon my arrival that consisted of a mix of professional and working-class adults. They were committed to the church and not necessarily following the personality of the previous leader. This meant that at the core of who we were was a traditional center that could be destroyed or built upon. We would decide to build upon this traditional core by inviting the staunch supporters of the church to come along with God's plan. The more traditional nature of the church wasn't frowned upon. Their attraction to me and my attraction to them was linked to this traditional identity, which wasn't inflexible but had potential to be the common denominator in the growth we would experience with inroads with the hip hop generation.

Prior to my call to the Mount, I was completing my seventh year as pastor of a growing church in York, Pennsylvania, and simultaneously completing a doctoral program. This is important, because as I completed my stay in York and my doctoral work, I was secure in who I was as a pastor. It is important for pastors to know who they are as they reach out to hip hop and lead a church. Clarification of values, principles, and leadership style is crucial. The completion of my doctoral program was a key ingredient in my being able to go to the Mount and be mature enough to see me in them and them in me. I wasn't afraid of the challenge but rather looked forward to what God was about to do through us. A good match of pastor to congregation is important when it comes to church growth and reaching the hip hop generation. There must be some common starting points between pastor and congregation that can guide the work they are to do together as they reach out to the hip hop generation.

The revelation of my leaving my former ministry and eventually accepting the call to the Mount was not an overnight experience. Though I don't have the time to give you the complete story, allow me to give you a glimpse of the process. After completing the doctorate, I was looking forward to settling into the pastorate in York and providing uninterrupted care for that congregation. I was surprised when the Lord began whisper to me that it may be time to leave and go to a new charge. After eleven months of praying and discerning, Mount Ararat called, and I and my family answered. In June 1997, my wife, I, and our daughter made the move from York to Pittsburgh.

When we got to Mount Ararat, we were greeted by approximately nine hundred faithful members who were excited about the church's future. Most of those members were over forty and had worked diligently to keep the church moving forward, supporting the programs and ministries the church provided to the congregation and the city. I embraced them, and they embraced me. We began to ascertain where they had been and where the Lord was leading us. It was obvious that I was younger than my congregation, and they and I knew that for the future of the church we were going to have to reach people in my age group and younger. We began to move in that vein, enlisting them in the process of reaching up to God and out to those we knew needed us and we needed them. We didn't abandon our strength or our core, but rather we built on it.

PAST, PRESENT, AND FUTURE TENSE: THE MOUNT ON THE MOVE

The process of change and growth that began in 1997 has blossomed over the past nine years of marriage between pastor and people. The church has experienced phenomenal growth. One of the things we have always done and continue to do is provide leadership to the East End section of Pittsburgh. In many cities across the nation, African American churches have been pressured to follow the exodus of middle-class African Americans to the suburbs. But in our case, we understood that the Mount was a rock that was called to stay put. While other churches moved out of the East End—which could be considered the inner city—we embraced this location. We have found that those who are attracted to the Mount don't fear or disdain our location. Instead, our location is a place of connection for them.

In many ways, being a black church in a predominantly African American community serves as a means for hip hoppers to return to their roots. Whether or not they were raised in the East End, to be back in what African Americans lovingly refer to as the 'hood has served as a positive for us. We also know that for hip hop—which is more activist-minded than actually activist—that to be a part of a church that is doing a lot with working-class, inner-city residents would be a way for hip hoppers to live out their commitment to make change. The hip hop generation wants this connection to inner-city ministry and community transformation, and it is a ministry that we lift up and celebrate with them. Many of them may be very busy with the demands of corporate America and/or rearing their young families, but via their tithes and offering and being connected to the Mount, they know they are making a difference. As much as the identity of the Mount has changed, the location has been a constant.

During the first year of my tenure at the Mount, we immediately began to attract young adults. The first response was obviously one of curiosity, as many came to see who followed my predecessor. Well, it was me standing there looking back at them while looking like them. I didn't have on baggy jeans, tee shirts, or chains; I had on either a robe or a very professional business suit. I reflected the younger part of my congregation while never leaving out the more senior members who had shown their commitment to the Mount and to me by extending a call to me to be their pastor. I respected the trust the senior members had placed in me, and I respected those things we had in common. As young adults began to come to the Mount, they not only saw a pastor who looked like them, but they also saw in our senior members what they hoped to become. They saw successful African Americans who had weathered the storms of life, pulpit leadership transition, and they were still standing strong and welcoming the young adults to be an active part of the life of the Mount. I can't underestimate how important the congregation and its leaders were in our growth. Without the congregation's loving embrace of me as their pastor and of the new members who were coming in to be a part of our lives, the growth would have been stifled.

As much as pastoral leadership is a key ingredient in reaching the hip hop generation, without the support of the larger congregation the move can prove most difficult. The new members wanted to feel accepted and welcomed. For them to feel accepted and welcomed had to be a joint effort between the pulpit and the pew. If people respond to the preached word and come down the aisle but aren't integrated into the life of the church in love, they will eventually leave that congregation. The congregation must be both supportive and involved in the effort to attract and keep young adults in the church.

FROM THE PULPIT TO THE CROSS: JESUS AS SAVIOR, NOT CELEBRITY

Let us return to the unique factors of the Mount. As I reflect on the unique factors that spurred our attracting young adults, I invite you to reflect upon those things that make your congregation unique. I firmly believe that each congregation has unique attributes that can be enhanced to attract that part of the hip hop generation that resonates with a specific congregational identity. While I don't consider myself hip hop or hip hoppish, I realize that I and the Mount feed into something that attracts hip hop. Hip hop likes celebrity. While I do not consider myself a celebrity or promote celebrity status, one thing about celebrity is that every celebrity personality is unique. If it is Diddy or Jay-Z, these brothers are unique as they embrace their roots or past to inspire their present. They dress the part, walk the walk, and talk the talk. They are models of what many of hip hop wants to become.

Much of hip hop wants to be professional. They want to wear suits and own businesses. Hip hop doesn't want to be on the grind in the streets. Hip hop wants to sit in the corner office and run the business. Damon Dash isn't unique; he is as hip hop as Young Jeezy. Hip hop is professional. I embraced my commitment to excellence and professionalism as rooted in my past to inspire my leadership and ministry at the Mount. The Mount is and was a church that has attracted a significant number of professionals. This professional identity and uniqueness was something we built upon.

The professional identity of the Mount, along with my identity as a called minister who was to be professional and all that I did, is rooted very much in my history as well. My connection with the identity of the Mount as a megaministry along with its being a countercultural professional ministry also has a common link with my past. I was mentored in a megachurch in Baltimore. Dr. Walter S. Thomas, the leader of New Psalmist Baptist Church, was and is one of my chief mentors. I was introduced to Dr. Thomas when I was fifteen. The discipleship thrust of that church and the magnetism of the pastor to attract young adult African American males was the ground that would become the foundation for my understanding of ministry. The ministry of that church promoted the kingdom of God as a counterculture to the age in which we were living. The kingdom was never presented as a reality that we fit our culture into; rather, the kingdom was presented as a reality that made us view ourselves as citizens of a heavenly sphere and therefore aliens in the culture.

As a young adult I wanted to hear about kingdom living. I knew how to live in the world and be worldly or down with the culture that was all around me, but how do I live counter to the culture? Dr. Thomas was teaching in touch with the culture, speaking and teaching with eloquence and relevance, but he was not selling out to the culture. He was talking about kingdom living. It was at New Psalmist that I found the answer to the questions I was raising about how I should live as a young African American male who didn't necessarily care to be taken in by the vices in the world that I thought weren't healthy or helpful. I sought to rid my life of practices that would tempt me to want to be more a part of the culture than of the kingdom. Rap was being birthed, and teenage activities included everything from partying to drugs, and I painfully sought to resist the temptations that I was facing daily. I went as far as refusing to listen to anything other than spiritual or religious music. I distanced myself from the house parties and surrounded myself with persons of like spiritual ambitions.

At the ripe old age of twenty-two, I started pastoring with a countercultural view in my head and heart. I had spent the last six years serving as an assistant under Dr. Thomas at New Psalmist. It is important to understand this context because it shaped the preaching and ministry model I later develop at the Mount. I didn't reject who I was or my desire to offer the world a viable biblical alternative to hip hop culture. I represented that increasing core of young adults who don't embrace all of hip hop or popular culture. We are looking for what God has to offer in a package that looks and sounds different from what bombards us day in and day out. Then and now I have little appreciation for or familiarity with much that exists in the hip hop culture. Most of my preaching lacks any of the language or content present in hip hop, and this helps to explain why young adults attend the Mount in such large numbers. They are looking for a church that represents *church*. Remember, the hip hop generation is not monolithic. There are many in hip hop who want the church to be that pillar that stands out in the world and culture as being different. Churches cannot be afraid to be that pillar that speaks back to hip hop culture in love, while not openly condemning it, but offering a biblical alternative and being unapologetically the church of Jesus Christ. This will not scare hip hop away from the church; it will attract a core of the hip hop generation that is looking for this as a way of being Christian.

I want to be clear that as much as I am not hip hop, I understand how being who I am touches on the professional side of hip hop culture. It is clear to me why so many of the hip hop generation embrace the ministry of the Mount. I am not running rappers down in my sermons. I am not condemning the worst of hip hop. What we are doing at the Mount is offering a godly example of how to be young, Christian, professional, successful, and faithful disciples. While I don't disparage how others are doing it, we found at the Mount that our unique way of reaching hip hop works for us. Churches don't have to become hip hop churches to reach hip hop. Churches have to be true to what they are called to be as God calls each church to reach parts of hip hop differently. When I reach out to hip hop in my preaching and teaching, everything that I am saying here informs what I am doing.

PREACHING TO HIP HOP: EXCELLENCE AND EXEGESIS

The approach I take to preaching to hip hop is one of excellence with quality exegesis. Let me reiterate: it is just as important to exegete one's culture as it is to exegete the text to be preached. In Pittsburgh, young adults have few options for social outlets, cultural connectivity, or mental engagement. The city has undergone a life-and-death experience. We had to ask the questions, as we exegete the city, how can we be a part of the cultural resurrection of Pittsburgh by being a religious center that offers an alternative to the culture? The Mount provides a place for many young adults in the city to gather and to be spiritually uplifted. In 2003, we started a Saturday evening service after being encouraged to do so by a guest preacher. After preaching for us one weekend, this pastor noted that if another service was not added, membership growth would start to stagnate. I knew I couldn't add another Sunday worship service. Preaching a fourth time on Sunday was not an option. We opted to try a Saturday service presented as an extra service for the summer. The sanctuary of the church, which seats fifteen hundred, was full the second Saturday after we started the "extra summer service."

What was unique about this Saturday service was that it was full of young adults. After careful consideration, it became clear that given the lack of social outlets in the city on a Saturday night, our church became the hang-out, and many used it as a meeting ground to determine where to go and what to do after service. While I will not try to negate the quality of the church's ministries, the power of the preaching ministry of the church, or the impact of its powerful worship, one of the reasons young adults attend in large numbers is because the church provides a gathering place. We came to understand that hip hop likes places to gather to meet, greet, and hang out. They needed a center to work from. We became that Saturday night center. We preached to them the gospel of Jesus Christ, no holds barred, and they responded and continue to respond. We point them to the cross with a powerful worship experience that speaks to all of their senses and calls for a response to the preached word.

We also found with this crowd of young adults that many were so immersed in the hip hop culture that church became the place to exhale from hip hop overdose. For a season I went through a period of trying to pepper messages with the language of the hip hop culture in an attempt to be relevant and to connect. After a Sunday service, a small group of young adults mustered the courage to come to the office and ask if they could have a few moments of the pastor's time. When we sat down to talk, I was shocked to hear that while I was attempting to be relevant and to connect, that was not why these young adults were attending. They expressed their excitement every weekend to get dressed and come to church because they knew they were going to hear something other than what they were being flooded with all week long. This provided a surprising education for me. I discovered that not every young adult was a hip hop lover or that those who had an appreciation for it did not want their lives saturated with it. That day I pledged to be the preacher of the "other world" gospel that had attracted him to the call of Christ years earlier in his own home church.

Mount Ararat today is full of young adults, many of whom are very appreciative of the cultural practices that dominate this season of our ministry. However, when they think of their spiritual lives they see Christ and the kingdom he offers as an alternative community. Maturity for them is shedding the trappings of the culture, and they do view the ministry of the church as being a place to support, defend, or teach the culture they are seeking to engage from a mature Christian perspective. We have found that many young adults see themselves growing up and moving father away from hip hop culture. They see the church as the laboratory for shedding the skin of hip hop culture in exchange for the "other world" demands of the kingdom. The Mount is helping them become what they want to become in a healthy way. We are not condemning hip hop culture, but we are offering a healthy, godly alternative.

The approach at the Mount is unique, but I would bet that there are many young adults in every city who would fit the profile of the young adults we are reaching. Young adults need options. They need to see churches that are relevant to them but not copycats of what they see in the world. They want alternatives. Churches have be willing to be what God has uniquely called them to be while not beating up on young adults and assuming that all of them have been taken hostage to hip hop culture. While all young adults have been touched by hip hop culture, they are not all consumed or totally in support of the culture. There is a large core of the hip hop generation that is looking for churches that resemble traditional churches, that do traditional with class and excellence. They are looking for relevant preaching that takes the Bible seriously and confronts worldly values by offering Christ-centered values. They are looking for churches that have powerful worship that is upbeat but not hip hop. Each congregation must find its way back to our young adults. In doing so, the church must realize that many young adults aren't asking the church to become like them; they want to become more like Christ.

CHAPTER 9

REAL BIG: THE HIP HOP PASTOR AS POSTMODERN PROPHET

OTIS MOSS III

"The Blues help you get out of the bed in the morning. You get up knowing you ain't alone. There's something else in the world.... This be an empty world without the Blues. I take that emptiness and try to fill it up with something."

—Ma Rainey, from *Ma Rainey's Black Bottom,* by August Wilson

The blues aesthetic described by Ma Rainey in August Wilson's play accurately describes the spiritual impulse vibrating through my life. The creative lens of the African American church has colored my spiritual worldview. Through this lens I witnessed the Western divisions of sacred and secular dissolve under the weight of the blues and gospel motif inherent in the African American religious tradition. "I take that emptiness and try to fill it up with something." I have attempted to fill this void with the eternal virtues rooted in Christ and shaped by my faith.

The sounds of John Coltrane's saxophone, James Baldwin's prose, Zora Neal Hurston's canonization of folk traditions, Fannie Lou Hamer's prophetic, political rhetoric, Martin Luther King's democratic Christian ideals, and Howard Thurman's Southern-inspired mysticism were the chords that composed the song of my spiritual journey within my household. My father and mother both are children of the South and products of the rich religious heritage of the African American church. Dr. Otis Moss Jr., my father, currently pastors in Cleveland, Ohio, and his church resonates with the Southern patterns of rhythmic speech and prophetic Christian witness drawn from the prophets Amos, Isaiah, and Jeremiah. This integration of prophetic imagination, worship, and ministry is a hallmark of my father's witness. Both of my parents were active in the freedom movement and brought to our family and church a rich and diverse ethic of liberation and redemption rooted in love. This unique narrative guided my spiritual formation.

On the surface, my family, church, and community might appear antithetical to the culture of hip hop, which was a dominant cultural force during my maturation into adulthood, but the politically inspired rhymes of Public Enemy and the cultural consciousness of A Tribe Called Quest along with KRS One found a resting place upon my spirit and helped me understand the world in which we live. The merging of hip hop culture, Christian witness, and liberation theology has been an enduring part of my ministry.

My matriculation at Morehouse College and seminary at Yale Divinity School solidified my interest in these two influential African American cultural products—which have mostly been at odds but desperately seek reconciliation. Morehouse College presented me with new methodological tools to examine an intellectual hunch and broadened my inquiry into the disciplines of cultural studies, economics, and political science. This broadened inquiry led to the discovery that I have termed the "Post-Soul Crisis in the Black Church." The underpinnings of my thesis state that hip hop culture and the generation that created it is the first generation of African American youth to develop and produce cultural products without explicit "soul sensibilities," or outside the black church. As a result, hip hop culture as an art form develops outside the faith-based ethics of the black church.

Soul culture, by contrast, is connected to the faith community. Soul culture produced Marvin Gaye, Aretha Franklin, Jackie Wilson, and Sam Cook, each of whom developed within the sacred confines of the black religious tradition. They brought their religious sensibilities or soul sensibilities to the marketplace. Post-soul culture was never nurtured in the womb of the black church, and as a result it nursed from the breast of market forces and morally ambiguous political ideology.

CHAPTER 9

For eight and a half years I pastored the Tabernacle Baptist Church in Augusta. The church went from 125 to 2,100 people, most of whom were from the unchurched and hip hop community. I viewed my role as prophetic interpreter, within the context of a traditional church, which was developing a hip hop/post-soul demographic. I started this work at twenty-six and was located within this generation, but I was also a post-civil rights child who was brought up in a prophetic black church pastored by my father and mentor, Otis Moss Jr. My role in this traditional church, Tabernacle, was to be a bridge between generations and a prophetic voice. I was called to be a prophetic cultural critic who could speak to multiple generations. This chapter will demonstrate, from a practical theological framework, how my church was transformed by God to become an intergenerational prophetic ministry connected to the hip hop community and the civil rights generation.

INTRODUCTION TO THE POST-SOUL WORLD

In 1987, the hip hop group Public Enemy utilized the sound of a prison escape siren in the opening of their concerts and the opening track of their second album. This sound would be a significant step in accessing the cultural shift that has taken place since "liberal integrationism" became the dominant ideology of "liberation" among mainstream black leadership. Public Enemy, on all of their albums, saw themselves as enemies of the system. The siren represented the need for oppressed groups, and black people in particular, to break out of the prison of American repression. This type of social critique—which views America as flawed at best and evil at worst—is a common theme in rap music. This type of subversive critique of the status quo is a long way from the soulful sound of Aretha Franklin, the calypso beats of Harry Belafonte, and the gospel-rooted, tenor voice of Marvin Gaye. Over the past thirty years, black America has undergone a dramatic shift politically and culturally. No longer is the church the central reference point for understanding black pain and suffering within the context of America. Secular-influenced, urban-based blues called hip hop now define the dilemma many black people are struggling to understand. Gone are the days of nonviolent direct action galvanized by the black church and revolutionary nationalist self-defense groups organized by black youth in the 1960s. Middle-class political legislative leadership has replaced community-based and religious activists as the dominant negotiating group with the power structure.

This new physical and cultural landscape has altered the demographic and economic face of black America in a way inconceivable thirty years ago. Whether this change is positive or negative is still up for debate, but without a doubt, black America must come to grips with its new self and attempt to understand it. The black middle class has increased, and more black students attend predominantly white institutions. Black middle-class parents for the first time in history can rear their children in exclusively white settings, raising new questions about the cultural and political demographics of twenty-first-century black leadership and strategies for liberation. We are at a unique time in the collective history of people of African descent. While the middle class is expanding and enjoying some of the fruits of the civil rights era's labor, the black working class and underclass are fighting for survival within deteriorating urban landscapes. The truth is that many people of color, especially youth, are fighting for survival and attempting to gather meaning out of this strange land called America. With the increase in police repression, demonization of people of color, introduction of crack cocaine, and the de-industrialization of urban centers, black people find themselves at a crossroads. Old tactics and strategies of change are now obsolete.

The term "post-soul," created by *Village Voice* writer Nelson George, best describes the present cultural position of black America. No longer are we based within a soul tradition that is implicitly and explicitly bound to the black Southern religious tradition defined by the institution we call the black church. Black America is now in a post-soul era. Black people exist in a radically different class and cultural structure. The gulf between the classes and the rise of hip hop music has changed the way the black community views itself.

The ghetto-centric, pain-filled lyrics of hip hop are truly the answer to Langston Hughes's question, "What happens to a dream deferred?" Hip hop culture is the dream deferred. It has dried up in the sun of a postindustrial, urban America and exploded upon the racist geography of American political ideology. It strikes fear and revulsion in the hearts of white America and simultaneously makes sense out of the absurd context of black suffering within urban areas. Hip hop is the new inner-city blues that makes everyone want to holler.

Hip hop is a black cultural form that attempts to define the nature of urban suffering. The dynamic contradictions and tensions that shape this urban cultural form confound and confuse many critics and historians who attempt to assess meaning from this unique post-soul phenomena. Many people from the Marxist point of view categorize hip hop as a cultural form connected to the economic factors of America. Other critiques have tried to place it as a continuation of an African oral tradition that has filtered into African American culture. Hip hop is actually located in both schools of thought. It is influenced by corporations' need for profit but simultaneously subverts white supremacist ideology by pointing out the contradiction in American society. A black cultural expression connected to the black oral and blues-based music traditions of the South, hip hop uses language and technology to entertain, critique, and define the urban centers from which it originates.

Hip hop is a means for young black men and women to define their reality. It gives value to their world, which has been defined by white culture as having no value. It may not always be positive or Afrocentric, but hip hop points to the problems in society that many black people have refused to address. The hip hop community recognizes the contradiction of urban existence and the fallacy of the American dream founded upon a system that exploits people of color. This is part of the positive side of hip hop, which acts as a cultural critic. This does not mean that hip hop is devoid of sexist and violent lyrics, which exploit women and, at times, glorify violence.

Hip hop's negative and sexist overtones do not come out of a vacuum. They are rooted within American culture, which teaches violence and disregard for women through talk shows, soap operas, and music videos. Black youth do not own Time-Warner, Sony, MCA, and Fox, which produce these shows and decide which artists will be played on the radio. Since hip hop is located in inner cities, it is subjected to and bombarded by a consumer culture, which defines status materially and personhood physically. The disturbing sexism in the music is an amplification of the sexism that is deeply rooted in American culture.

The problem perceived by white America is that rap music disrupts the boundaries that racism sets up to demonize black culture. When white youth begin buying rap music and using its vernacular in their homes, rap music becomes sexist and violent. White mainstream media attack rap music because it has entered middle-class suburbia. The objectifying of women in Hollywood films, television, and white mainstream churches is seen as normal, but the lyrics of black youth are seen as an evil scourge that must be wiped out by the vanguards of white culture. This selective criticism is the heart of racist criticism of hip hop music that must view black and other colored people as evil, sexually deviant, exotic, violent, childlike, and dangerous in order to maintain supremacy. Hip hop music is the inner-city griot of today. We must first listen to its message and try to understand our youth before condemning them. They are truly singing a new inner-city blues, but before we holler, we must first seek understanding.

FRESH WATER FROM OLD WELLS

> When the people saw that Moses was so long in coming down from the mountain, they gathered around Aaron and said "Come, make us gods who will go before us. As for this fellow Moses who brought us up out of Egypt, we don't know what has happened to him." (Exodus 32:1 NIV)

CHAPTER 9

The scenario of the golden calf goes to the heart of the post-soul crisis in black America. Moses, the anointed the leader of the Hebrews, stands upon Mount Sinai communing with God. As he stands visually and physically cut off from the congregation, a cadre of "church people" gathers before Aaron and makes a demand of the interim pastor. A voice from the crowd is heard echoing the desires of the collective body: "Make us gods who will go before us!...Make us gods who will not demand wilderness wanderings or erect moral boundaries in a wilderness world where morality is elusive and ethical constructs are relative." Aaron creates and canonizes the world's first prosperity ministry: a god the people can control and chose how to engage.

The irony of the story is that the golden calf was made from material or residue given to the people by God as they left Egypt. They took their earrings, chains, gold, silver, and other jewelry and began to worship and bow to the material/residue as if it were the source of life and cosmological power. Is this not strange: a people who witnessed the works of Yahweh and could testify to the awesome power flowing from the mouth of God decide to bow to ancient monetary forms of exchange? This story illustrates the real danger of postmodern society: the proclivity to elevate the material, in the words of Paul Tillich, to an "ultimate concern" through the creation of rituals and doctrines that point to market forces as the salvation for all spiritual and physical ills. The people invented a god, controlled this god, and had no moral or ethical obligations associated with this new god. Postmodern culture disrupts all notions of truth through deconstruction and replaces it with "Keep it Real" slogans. The ground of moral reality is rooted in one's ability to stay true to whatever moral code has been designed by one's cultural context. The moral boundary is rooted in "if it feels good" or if the market can tolerate it, then do it; if not, cease. This is part of the danger of hip hop/post-soul culture. For those of you with an old-school cultural understanding, please do not misunderstand this statement. Hip hop is a viable, brilliant, artistic cultural production, and at times a revolutionary art form, but when it is wedded to the modern market forces and demonized by conservative Christian theology, it drifts toward the moral absurdity of the larger society.

Modern American culture, in this context, is a golden calf cutting urban youth and the post-soul culture off from its roots, rituals, and life-sustaining beliefs. If the culture of the calf is allowed to remain, a generation will develop with a "bling-bling equals blessing" mentality, to quote Dr. Jeremiah Wright Jr. of Trinity United Church of Christ. We understand, based on the text, that the calf is destroyed and Golden Calf Ministries closes its doors forever. What would happen, I wonder, if the congregation were allowed to exist and produce mega-calf ministries with the same theological, ideological foundations?

Over the last fifty years, we have witnessed the rise of the golden calf. If America's highest value is not constitutional freedoms but free markets, we are living in an age of the golden calf. Since the mid-1960s, America has witnessed rapid changes in modes of production, information, and technology. America as a whole has become more segmented and insular, and it has embraced a customized approach to economic and civic engagement. Modern households now have, regardless of income, at least two televisions with at least thirty channels. With the rise of customized television choice, family conversation decreases to make space for individual entertainment choices. The normal ritual of family meals, conversation, imagination, and riding in the car together has been displaced. The family trip in the car has been turned into a customized entertainment experience. Every member of the family has the option of headphones for music or DVDs of choice. As the Internet expands and more homes are online, isolation becomes the normal routine of the house; surfing the Net, watching the news, or putting on headphones to listen to the latest MP3 downloads is now the norm. There is no need to compromise or negotiate space or collectively discover activities. The market has given us the ability to choose what the individual wants above the ethic of the family. The world of hip hop did not invent this new culture, but it exists as a critic and addict of postmodern sensibilities.

What does all this cultural criticism have to do with the church and worship and hip hop culture? As Lauryn Hill stated several years ago, "Everything!" A family rooted in post-soul culture and influenced by hip hop comes to church with post-soul sensibilities. Television has effectively trained the minds of two or three generations that all problems should or can be solved in thirty minutes or an hour. MTV-inspired filmmaking style, popularized by Hype Williams, Paul Hunter, and Michael Bay, demand quick cuts for a short-attention-span audience. This is the background a post-soul community brings to church in the twenty-first century.

The strength of the church—particularly the black church—when rooted in a liberation ethic is revolutionary transformation through Christ. The church is one of the only places where the people are forced to struggle together in community and come to grips with the message of a Savior who demands not personal salvation but community transformation. "The Spirit of the Lord is on me, because he has anointed me to preach good news to the poor. He has sent me to proclaim freedom for the prisoners and recovery of the sight for the blind, to release the oppressed, to proclaim the year of the Lord's favor" (Luke 4:18-19 NIV). We engage each other through prayer, congregational songs, passing of the peace, collective giving, and a community call and response, rooted in the African tradition.

According to liturgical scholar Robert Webber, "Worship is a verb," a celebratory act, event, and community engagement. In order to bring fresh water to the old well of the African American church, we must reassess our theology of worship, or in some cases, develop a theology of worship, which celebrates Christ but also engages the post-soul community.

MODES OF WORSHIP IN THE AFRICAN AMERICAN CHURCH

Worship in the African American community has always been dynamic and fluid. Our historical struggles, socioeconomic status, and theological reflection are woven into the fabric of African

American religious experience. But a brief look at the development of the middle-class models of worship in the African American community can help us understand why they are not equipped to reach the hip hop community. The African American church, according to scholar Melville J. Herskovits, is a matrix of African rituals, beliefs, and values infused with the unique American experience of slavery and liberation ethic of the gospel.[1] The church has been and is a sacred space of creative freedom and imagination. The black church historically has been the place where men and women of color could be full human beings away from the oppressive, watchful eyes of "slave masters."

The majority of African American institutions find their genesis in the womb of the church: black colleges, black insurance companies, the civil rights movement, civic organizations, and labor unions. The black church is critical to our understanding of black cultural productions such as blues, jazz, spirituals, linguistic nuances, and political ideologies of the black community. This "invisible institution" or faith community developed on plantations, near streams, and around hidden fields in the place where people of African descent reflected theologically on their collective experience of pain in America. The earliest independent black churches are Silver Bluff Baptist in Silver Bluff, South Carolina, Africa Baptist in Mecklenburg, Virginia, and First African in Savannah, Georgia. The dates of establishment range from 1773 to 1788. What must be noted about these churches is their move from invisible institutions to a visible institution. The church was now prone to institutionalize Southern social forces, which would create acceptance and rejection of different worship styles.

Most scholars agree that during the 1700s to 1800 many black churches from the Baptist tradition exemplified a worship style that could be connected to their West African roots. African chants, metered music, spirituals, and praise hymns were the norm. Call and response worship services sprinkled with events called "catching the Holy Ghost" or "getting happy" was normative. The era of Reconstruction brought a change in African American worship. As men and women found a degree of mobility in the segregated South, African-influenced modes of worship, singing, communication, and socialization were rejected by the growing black middle class. The call and response, spirituals, African chants, and ring shouts of the earlier generations were looked down on by the new "reconstructionist middle class." Many churches founded in the 1700s and 1800s were called First African or Second African. But during this period through the early part of the twentieth century, with the rise of this new middle class that was seeking acceptance in the larger society, the word *African* was dropped from the religious vocabulary.

With the increasing stratification between rural and urban worshipers, which was intensified by the culture of classism, worship changed rapidly in the black church. Churches now defined themselves not only by denomination but also by class, and in some cases, by color. "Educated" people who were trained from the Eurocentric perspective populated many middle-class churches, especially those from predominantly white denominations. European anthems, hymns, and liturgy were appealing to these congregants. The modes of worship associated with Africa and the fields of the South were rejected for a more European paradigm of worship. This is the beginning of what many of us call the "traditional church." By *traditional* we mean a church with at least two of the following:

1. It is at least one hundred years old.
2. It is rooted in music from the 1940s to the 1960s.
3. It rejects Africanized modes of worship.
4. The members' average age is between fifty-five and sixty-five.
5. It has a Eurocentric model of worship.

These churches looked toward the broader culture to validate their existence. The African American Baptist tradition developed into three distinct trajectories. The first was the middle-class Baptist church. This church had a trained or educated clergy and a large educated laity. Education was extremely important and viewed as the ticket to upward mobility. These congregations valued college education and encouraged many of their high school students to further their education. The paradox was that this congregation, in general, was hostile to Africanized worship in the church: call and response, Spirit possession, improvisation in liturgy, spirituals, common meter hymns, and other creative tensions in worship. They tended to valorize strict liturgy, downplayed call and response, and rejected Spirit possession and any form of worship and preaching that connected the church to its African roots.

The second trajectory in the Baptist church was made up of working-class people and/or working poor, who embraced the Africanisms but had a proclivity to reject social engagement. The final trajectory was the move toward a Holiness doctrine. This doctrine developed in working-class churches where black people were rejected by the larger society and felt the scorn of middle-class black people who looked down upon store-front communities of faith. Out of this alienation a new approach to worship was born. From this matrix came a focus on change of one's lifestyle and the separation from all forms of secular engagement.

The Pentecostal tradition in the African American church was born in the disruptive and depressing waters of the Civil War. Following the Civil War, former enslaved Africans and displaced Europeans attempted to find meaning in the postwar landscape of the South and North. The National Holiness Association, which began holding meetings in the 1860s in Vineland, New Jersey, answered the painful questions these wounded men and women had in the aftermath of the horrific Civil War and the demise of the agricultural economy in the South. The doctrine of the early Holiness movement stated that Christians were to be in the world and not of it. The early meetings were sponsored by Methodists who sought to live out John Wesley's idea of structured spiritual development, and the theology of the Pentecostal movement is rooted partly in Methodist doctrine and partly in African-inspired modes of worship and theological reflection. African American Pentecostalism would transform the doctrine of Holiness into a worldwide phenomenon.

CHAPTER 9

Two towering figures shaped the Pentecostal movement in America: William Seymour and Charles H. Mason. William Seymour was exposed to the doctrine of Holiness in Ohio at the Evening Lights Saints Church (also known as the Church of God). He found the doctrine appealing and was moved to share the doctrine with others. He took classes at God's Bible School in Cincinnati, Ohio, and later moved to Houston, Texas, to pastor. Seymour preached a gospel that saw no racial boundaries and lifted up the power of divine healing and sanctification. This pastorate was short-lived, but his next stop would give birth to the modern Holiness/Pentecostal movement in the West.

Seymour moved to California and began holding meetings at Bonnie Brae Street in Los Angeles in 1906. The gatherings became too large for this venue and moved to an old church once owned by an AME congregation at 312 Azusa Street, where many people were converted to the doctrine of sanctification. This revival lasted for weeks, and these Spirit-filled meetings attracted black, white, and Latino people. Seymour was deliberate in developing a diverse leadership team of men, women, black, white, and Latino. He firmly believed the Holy Spirit had the power to break down the barriers of class and race. His dream rang true until racism reared its ugly head and Holiness leaders and Los Angeles civic leaders banded together to disrupt the Azusa movement.

Charles H. Mason, a Baptist preacher born in Memphis, Tennessee, in 1866, would intersect with the teachings of Seymour. Mason began teaching the Holiness doctrine at Tabernacle Baptist Church in Alabama by teaching the need of people of faith to develop a new lifestyle in Christ. As the church grew, Mason spread the doctrine of Holiness, but he had not yet been "baptized in the Holy Spirit." In 1906, Mason made the decision to take his followers to Los Angeles to Azusa Street to gain some knowledge of this new revival movement led by Seymour. Upon his arrival, Mason was given the gift of the "Holy Spirit baptism."

This history must be mentioned because what we call Pentecostalism is nothing more than a matrix of African-inspired religious ritual. African-inspired Pentecostals, or the Spirit-led church, had several identifying motifs near the turn of the twentieth century:

1. Spirit baptism
2. Rejection of the world
3. African-inspired chants and moans
4. Afrocentric worship, Eurocentric-influenced theology

POST-SOUL WORSHIP

The question for traditional churches is how we develop a worship theology that is true to our roots culturally and relevant to the needs of the hip hop generation. We have seen the dangers of this new world and its values—background we need to develop a post-soul worship paradigm. Isaiah gives us some theological footing when he states, "See, I am doing a new thing!" The prophet was communicating to the people the sovereignty and mystery of God. The people of Israel were unfaithful to the history and tradition of the Mosaic law. As a result of their disobedience, they were placed in exile. During the exile, their houses of worship were assimilated into the majority culture. Once assimilated, they lost their prophetic edge to speak truth to power. The prophet Isaiah declares that God will step outside the traditional boundaries and save his people.

This new thing we speak of is more than praise and worship and beyond music. It is a systematic analysis of traditional/Eurocentric worship and modern culture. I believe every church, if it is serious about ministry in a postmodern age, can transform its worship to reach the hip hop generation.

Principles of Worship

Worship is the one thing the church should do very well. We are not arguing for monolithic worship, but that all worship should celebrate the Christ event and move us toward a deeper relationship with God. If this is not happening, then we are not living out our mission.

African American worship and preaching are characterized by the idea of celebration. Since the inception of the North American church, Africans in America have celebrated the Christ event. We have, as a people, celebrated who Christ is historically, what he is for us in the present, and what Christ will do in the future. Theologian James Evans states, "The two stubborn facts of African-American Christian existence are that God has revealed God's self to the black community and that this revelation is inseparable from the historic struggle of black people for liberation."[2]

African American faith has always wrapped its worship experience in the existential and eschatological. In other words, we have always worshiped with one foot in the soil of our present pain and another foot in our future hope. The blues music of the South is an example of a cultural production that looks at the community's present situation. The spirituals, by contrast, look at the world through the eyes of a liberating God: "Tell old Pharaoh to let my people go!" This song is not just a retelling of a biblical story but also a theological metaphor of what enslaved Africans wanted and would eventually receive through revolt, protest, and self-denial with and through Christ. A worship experience must take into account this history and celebrate the Christ event. The entire liturgy should lead the worshiper to a greater understanding of the radical nature of Jesus. The hip hop community wants to know "Why is Christ so great?" "What has he done?"

Many churches, however, have no celebrative aspect. We sing, pray, and preach with no energy, passion, or excitement. I was in a worship experience not long ago that was rigidly timed. I was the guest preacher and the church was without a pastor. The chairman of the deacon board informed me, "Reverend, we have doctors, judges, lawyers, and teachers. We are the leading church in this community!" (I thought to myself, Does anybody know Jesus? If this is the leading church, who is racing? Is there a weekly posting in the paper on which church is ahead this week?) He continued to inform me how the church did not like emotion but preferred content in sermons and was used to a one-hour service. I sat in the pulpit and observed the choir rush through a hymn, the deacons rush through tired prayers, and announcements get rushed. After one more rushed song, I preached. And I took my time. After the sermon came an invitation that lasted fifteen to twenty seconds. Visitors were welcomed and a benediction pronounced. I was blown away by the addiction to be out of service within fifty-five minutes. This congregation was not celebrating Christ but going through the motions!

Principles for Worship Transformation

The worship experience, even if there is no preaching, should point a guest toward Christ. Does your church celebrate Christ even if there is no preaching or singing? Can people recognize your mission? Every church should begin the celebration when people come into the parking lot. Parking lot greeters should be stationed to let people know the kind of church they are about to attend: one that cares. Once in the building, a welcome ministry stationed around the facility should again demonstrate the love of Christ to all who come in to his house.

Building and grounds. A neglected area among many churches is the facilities. A poorly kept facility says more about the congregation than good preaching or a hot choir. If you have been living with cracks in the walls and worn carpet, you will get used to it. No church should be poorly kept. We are maintaining God's house, and the carpet, lights, bathrooms, walls, and so on should be clean. It is a good idea to bring in a nonmember to give you an honest assessment of your church.

Art and symbolism. Every church, whether you meet in a school or cathedral, should display appropriate symbolism to usher people into the presence of God. Pictures of the former pastors, deacons, and other people are nice in a designated historical area but should not be the main feature in the worship center. If a person visiting your church sees twelve pictures of deceased members in the sanctuary and no symbols pointing to Christ, that person concludes that this is a historic church that loves its past but is not sure of its future.

Afrocentric art. No African American church in the twenty-first century should be without Afrocentric art. The foyer, fellowship hall, classrooms, worship center, and hallways should reflect the rich, diverse heritage of our community. I am sure at least one person reading this is saying, "Why does it matter? We're all the same in God's eyes." This is true, but African American children and adults are bombarded with images that perpetuate ungodly, racist, and destructive stereotypes. The church should be the place where children of color see themselves in a positive light. It is critical that the church place symbols, artifacts, and photographs that show African people as a part of the ancient biblical world. Christ should never be depicted as a European in a black church but at the least Afro-Asiatic! His disciples should be viewed in a variety of dark and light hues reflective of the ancient world they occupied. Hip hop has already embraced the historically accurate depiction of Christ. Just take a moment to listen to Talib Kweli, Mos Def, Common, KRS One, and the Wu-Tang Clan; they all speak of Jesus as a black man and make fun of churches and preachers who attempt to justify a European image of Christ. For those who are not convinced this is needed, I suggest reading Chiek Anta Diop, Dr. Charles Copher, Dr. Jeremiah Wright Jr., Kelly Brown Douglas, and Dr. Obery Hendricks to gain a background on these issues. Not only the pastor but the servant leaders of the church should examine these areas as well.

A FOUNDATION FOR POST-SOUL WORSHIP

What principles must be in place to lead this new generation of seekers to Christ in the context of worship? Pastor and teacher Carlyle Fielding Stewart gives three essential principals for growth of a church in the African American community:[3]

1. The worship experience should celebrate the life in Christ.
2. The worship service should inform people about God's wondrous and creative activity in the world.
3. The worship event should invite people into the fellowship of believers.

I believe Stewart is on target with these ideas. Several points should be added when a church is seeking to reach the post-soul or hip hop generation:

Ethics of Post-Soul Worship
- Celebration
- Information
- Inspiration
- Improvisation
- Invitation
- Using the pillars of hip hop culture to minister

These are the areas worshipers of the post-soul culture are looking for within the worship experience. They are not looking for just praise and worship or contemporary gospel; they want answers to the difficult questions.

Celebration

The act of worship is a divine drama in which the congregation is the cast, and the ministers, choir, worship leader, multimedia crew, ushers, deacons, and other lay leaders are stagehands. Recognizing this simple fact is essential to the growth and development of the church.

Many traditional churches in the African American community are in decline not because they don't have the anointing of God upon them but because they have lost their passion to celebrate Christ and recognize cultural changes. Why would a young person, struggling to understand life, want to sit for close to two hours in a church that has no passion for Christ and is afraid to speak with a prophetic voice? We must be clear on this: the hip hop generation sees people with passion and conviction all the time. Hip hop artists are passionate about their music. DJs are passionate about developing a new mix and sample. Hustlers are passionate about keeping it real on the street and promoting their product. Lawyers are passionate about their cases in court. Activists are passionate about the issues they champion. The church, beyond all others, has someone named Christ to be passionate about, but many of our traditional churches have lost all sense of passion. Only when passion is rekindled can celebration truly take place.

Does your worship experience celebrate Christ with a joyful tone, or is the mood, ethos, and culture somber? This generation is demanding a celebration ethic.

Post-Soul Test

(This may be the hardest part for seasoned pastors and lay leaders.)

1. If your church is lacking youth and young adult involvement, ask people in the age range who do not attend, "Why don't you attend?" (Don't ask your friends or family; they will not tell you the truth!)
2. Survey at least twenty-five people in this age range.
3. Do not argue or defend your church; just accept what they say.
4. Have the leaders of the church perform the same survey.
5. Ask your youth to engage in the same survey.
6. Compile the answers and find key words that keep coming up.
7. Meet with the leaders and discuss the results.

Information

The African American church has always been more than what Western theologians have defined as church. Church within the context of the African American community is and has been a way of life and a source of life-affirming information. Many modern churches have moved away from the information motif, which undergirded the African American church, and replaced it with a praise paradigm that is heavy on music but low on life-affirming information. This phenomenon is not new but has taken on a sinister characteristic as more untrained and some trained clergy have adopted a materialistic gospel that refuses to engage the critical issues facing the new generation.

What is needed in this age are men and women willing to proclaim the gospel with prophetic voices.

Information—life-affirming information—is vital to the survival of the African American community. This generation needs knowledge and the wisdom to apply this information. Information about Africa, HIV/AIDS, drug addiction, domestic violence, economic injustice, developing nonviolent relationships, sex, racism, sexism, hypersexuality, health, diet, financial planning, anger management, commitment, forgiveness, salvation, the importance of reading black and African history—these are some of the issues the church must address with authority. Life-affirming information is essential if we are to see a change in our community. What issues have been addressed in your church? Was the person addressing these issues knowledgeable?

As church leaders, we must be willing to engage and deal with tough issues. We cannot just support an opinion, but we must research (this means more than two books) a subject and find the pro and con perspectives. When we are not knowledgeable about an area, we should give way to a professional, and it should be made clear from the pulpit, "I defer to Dr. Smith, who is an expert on hypertension." When we are willing to present life-affirming information to God's people, we follow the path of the Old Testament prophets who sought to heal the people with God's anointed information.

Inspiration

Worship is anchored in art and it should inspire people to think critically and take action. We are called to celebrate and inform, but with no inspiration, our celebration becomes a ritual of obligation with no relevance to contemporary society. Often, because seminary has done a poor to mediocre job of preparing ministers for worship, we mistake music and call and response for inspiration. (Please do not misunderstand; inspirational music is needed, and call and response is necessary, and I am an advocate for seminary. But most seminaries do not have professors in the area of African American worship.)

A post-soul worship experience must inspire people to have a closer walk with God. It should arouse a spiritual yearning in the soul to deepen one's relationship with Christ, community, and culture. When inspiration is evident in worship, it energizes the entire fellowship to find their spiritual gifts and use them for the glory of the kingdom.

Does your worship experience inspire people to move closer to Christ? Does the preaching demand that people critically examine their lives and social structures? Does the music connect with the congregation's experience in the world and offer a theological alternative? Do the mood, ethos, and language of the worship cause people to reflect and rejoice?

We must first understand that music is memory to people. If you play A Tribe Called Quest's "Low End Theory," I can tell you when I first heard it and my reaction to these distinctive lyrics. If I play Sarah Vaughn, Stevie Wonder, Marvin Gaye, Luther Vandross, Brian McKnight, or Chris Brown to a variety of people, they will associate a time and place with the music. Music in the church context, though it has the high calling to illuminate Christ, also is trapped by the cultural memory of the congregation. When a person says, "I don't like that song," he or she is really saying, "That song invokes no memory for me." The songs we like in church are associated with memory and events: our baptism, Mom's funeral, Uncle Joe's devotion time, or Grandma singing around the house. The clash between generations is as much about new and old memories as it is about methodology.

In order to combat this clash of ideas, we must build a theology of worship with an ethic of inspiration. The sad truth is that many traditional churches believe God can speak only through a hymn or an anthem, and our contemporary churches feel the Holy Spirit moves only through gospel music. Music done well with the ethic of inspiration demands that we use what will undergird the Word, regardless of style.

The worship experience should flow theologically and/or liturgically. If the hymns, anthems, gospel, praise songs, and liturgical dance all lead and support the Word being presented, we reduce the friction in the worship experience. I believe the minister of music should know several weeks in advance what the minister will be preaching in order to prepare. When the music ministry is clear on the theological purpose, we reduce the tendency to pick music based on what we like or is familiar, and instead we can choose based on theology. When we try to lead people to Christ, our music must support the theological content and celebrative movements of the sermon.

This ethic of inspiration extends to other areas of worship as well. Worship becomes inspiring when we can see evidence of God at work. Allowing a person once addicted to crack to read the Scripture or a young person welcome the visitors lets the congregation develop a narrative of inspiration. They can say, "God is doing a mighty work with us because Mr. Smith is free from crack!" or "Did you hear the Jones girl? She has overcome her speech impairment." The pastor should make space for people in the body of Christ to share or demonstrate how God has healed, transformed, and convicted them. This does not mean a testimony hour, but let others besides the clergy participate in liturgy.

Inspiration can be found, most importantly, in Scripture. The Word should be read with authority and conviction. Ministers and laypersons should practice reading God's Word. The way we read Scripture can, at times, prevent people from hearing God's voice because we destroy the context and subtext with our poor reading. Every level of worship from music to preaching to Scripture and prayer should lead worshipers closer to Christ and inspire them to walk with the Savior.

Improvisation

An African American church without the ethic of improvisation is like Miles Davis without a trumpet. Something is missing when one is taken from its natural family. The ability to improvise allows the body of Christ to participate in the act of God's grace and revelation. African culture works under the assumption that God is constantly at work. If God is constantly at work we can't contain God or constrict God in preformatted structure that doesn't leave room for God to act improvisational in worship. Christ is the living embodiment of his divine action. When Christ engages suffering, pain, anger, or immorality, he never deals with these issues in an identical manner. There is no set liturgy. Legislative groups during Christ's day attempted to contain the divine within a set liturgy, doctrine, and tradition. The ethic of improvisation allows the worship experience to always dance on the edge of creative tension and divine imagination.

Improvisation is not the absence of structure and preparation; it is the inclusion of divine mystery in the worship experience. Improvisation says we leave space for God moving beyond and outside our plans. Jazz utilizes improvisation, but not at the expense of preparation. The democratic character of jazz leaves a space for each musician to express his or her gifts within the musical performance. The theme, purpose, and intent stay intact, but the road the musicians travel to arrive at their goal may vary from performance to performance. Worship should explore this tension and be daring enough to walk down different paths.

Euro-American religious practice has typically shunned or misunderstood this religious practice among Africans in North America. The early slave-holding Christians thought this form of improvisation was thoughtless, primitive, and childlike. What our European brethren failed to understand was the discipline, depth of creativity, and preparation required to truly open one's spirit to divine improvisation.

Does your church worship allow for songs to be stretched, deleted, or added in the worship experience? Can your liturgy be altered? Churches rooted in the traditional attempt to stick to liturgy with religious reverence, and any outbreak of the Spirit is quickly extinguished. I heard an elder pastor state to a group of young ministers, "At my church we do all things in order.... Everything is timed, and the people know we do not do all that 'carrying-on.' You young preachers like to encourage shouting. We worship with dignity at my church!" One of my colleagues quickly said to me, "They worship with dignity and empty pews!" This exchange is not uncommon, and on the surface it is the typical clash of generations. But deeper examination will reveal it is a rebellion against European religious values that dominate many middle-class and traditional mainline black churches.

Post-Soul Test

1. Does your music ministry ever change rehearsed songs in the middle of worship to connect with the climate and atmosphere of worship?
2. How do you react when the worship experience moves outside the scheduled liturgy?
3. Does your church encourage improvisation?
4. Have you personally experienced a moment in public worship where God changed your plans?

Invitation

> "Therefore go and make disciples of all nations, baptizing them in the name of the Father and of the Son and of the Holy Spirit, and teaching them to obey everything I have commanded you." (Matthew 28:19-20 NIV)

All we do in worship hinges on the act of invitation. Our primary task is to welcome and invite people to become a part of the body of Christ. A church that does not welcome and invite fails to live out the teachings of Christ. The act of invitation mistakenly has been left to the end of the service as an afterthought. The phrase "the doors of the church are open" resonates with many connected to the Baptist tradition, but it is not enough. In order to become a church that is inviting, the whole congregation must develop an attitude of welcome and invitation.

Too many traditional churches operate as a social club and create criteria for potential members. I recall an experience with a member of Tabernacle who indicated she "met a new doctor in town, and she was the type of person the pastor and deacons should recruit." The woman who made this statement is a wonderful person but had adopted the myth that this congregation should recruit a certain kind of people. This statement has problems on two levels. First is the idea that a certain kind of person with a particular vocation should be recruited by the church. This type of mentality must be removed completely from the church. This paradigm breeds class and socioeconomic conflict, not to mention that it is nonbiblical and runs counter to any form of liberation theology preached from the pulpit.

The second problem with the woman's statement is the belief that evangelism is the job of the pastor and deacons. When the congregation operates from the premise that all ministry, evangelism, and visitation is only the job of the pastor, the congregation is reduced to an audience that sits in the pews waiting for the show—starring the pastor—to begin. It is the job of the pastor to "equip the saints" for recruiting. Every person must view himself or herself as a disciple of Christ and minister to God's people. This idea will become a part of the congregation through structured teaching by the pastor. The pastor is key in transforming the culture of a congregation.

To create an environment of invitation, the first person to be assessed is the pastor. If the pastor has a reserved, closed, stand-offish, unfriendly spirit, the congregation will adopt the same spirit. It is important for ministers to do a personal inventory of their personality: Are you formal or laid back? Do you smile often, or are you reserved? Do you have a naturally humorous personality? Every pastor must understand his or her spirit if the spirit of a traditional church is to be changed to make room for the hip hop generation.

Invitation is intentional, not accidental. The worship experience should intentionally make people feel welcome. Music, passing of the peace, announcements, worship program—all avenues of worship should be viewed from the perspective of a visitor or guest. Is our program easy to follow? Are our rituals explained? Does our music ministry inspire, inform, and celebrate? Are our ushers friendly? Do trustees and deacons carry the spirit of the pastor, or will a guest receive one perspective from the pastor and another from the lay leaders? Is the invitation an afterthought, or do the music ministry, pastor, and lay leaders work as a team at this great moment? Invitation is important for a church to live out the message and teachings of Christ.

Another aspect of invitation overlooked is the aspect of dress for this generation. Many traditional churches have developed a reputation as fashion shows on Sunday. On one level this generalized criticism is true and false. Many black churches developed the tradition of wearing their Sunday best from Southern culture. African Americans in the South during the antebellum period were required to wear uniforms and work clothes all week except Sunday. Sunday became a day when we could dress without being required to look a certain way by our enslavers. This practice has continued till this day.

Today's culture presents new challenges to church etiquette. If a young person is unable to purchase a suit and tie, we create a class barrier to church attendance. Those from the corporate culture also acknowledge this aspect. Persons operating five days a week in the offices of American corporate culture are required to dress in the corporate uniform (suit and tie). Creating a church environment where those who have financial challenges along with those from the corporate culture can worship in a relaxed atmosphere is important. Those who choose to worship in suits should be comfortable with those who worship in slacks or jeans. The world demands deconstruction of traditions that present barriers to worship.

Post-Soul Test

1. Does your church currently have a welcome ministry or greeters in place?
2. If not, why not?
3. Are lay leaders trained on how to welcome people to and at church?
4. Does your church dress formally (suit, tie, etc.)?
5. If yes, why?

The Pillars of Hip Hop for Church Transformation

Tricia Rose, a former professor at New York University, has written an excellent academic treatment of hip hop culture, *Black Noise*.[4] In her book she identifies the origins of hip hop: it began in 1972 in the

South Bronx with a DJ named Kool Herc who had only two turntables and a microphone to get the party started. Urban youth in the Bronx did not have the money for guitars, drums, and other instruments, so they appropriated the available technology and baptized it in the waters of black imagination. This is how hip hop was born in the womb of urban decay and youth-inspired imagination.

Now I know what some of you are saying: "We will have no hippy hop in God's church. There will be no rapping in God's house!" (Read the sentence out loud with a hoarse and rough preacherly voice to get the full effect of the statement.) But hip hop is more than rap, beats, and cussing (thank you very much). An overview of hip hop culture demonstrates that it has four pillars:

1. Rap
2. DJing
3. Break dancing
4. Graffiti

In order to understand these four bases of hip hop, we must examine the universal side of each pillar. First, rap is nothing more than oral communication and poetry. In an age where young people need to develop their verbal skills, it would be foolish for the church to shun poetry. The Bible is filled with poetic images, and the church can use poetry, rhyme, and story telling to reach this generation. Create space in your church where youth can recite Langston Hughes, Common, and Jill Scott. Allow young people to use their oral skills to expound upon a specific topic like poor education as a "Weapon of Mass Destruction" or HIV and AIDS. Please remember, many black preachers rap and rhyme when they get to the end of a sermon—it is called a whoop!

DJing is just an appropriation of technology. This generation is not technophobic, and they have the skills to use current technology effectively. Stop asking an ancient deacon to run the sound and media ministry. If you can't program TIVO or a DVD player, you should not be in charge of technology. Screens, podcasts, MP3s, iPods, and blogs are normal forms of communication. This generation raises questions when they don't see a community of faith using the latest technology.

Maybe you're now saying you get the first two pillars, but "you must be crazy if you think some 'b-boy' is going to spin on his head during the processional!" Well, you don't need to have anyone spin on his or her head, but we should note that when we say break dance we are talking about movement. Psalm 150 states, "Praise the Lord with the dance [movement]." Seventy percent of all communication is nonverbal! Imagine how we can communicate to this generation if we allow creative uses of movement and dance in the worship experience. A ministry of dance and step should be created to teach teamwork, discipline, and the sacredness of the human body.

The final pillar, graffiti, on the surface, seems to have no theological implications. I can hear a seasoned preacher stating, "There is no way I will let God's church be vandalized by 'grow-footy' artists." The central word to focus on is art. Graffiti has been one of the most influential street media of the last twenty years. Japanese animators have borrowed from hip hop culture to create new cartoon characters, and Aaron McGruder, the creator of "The Boondocks" comic strip, has been influenced by graffiti. The church has had a history of using graffiti. We just have a nice-sounding name for it: stained glass windows. The symbols and icons in many churches started out as street art that was eventually legitimized by the Roman Catholic Church. What would happen in your church if you allowed youth and young adults to create original works of art for the sanctuary or for a special sermon series? At my former and current church, artists in residence create artwork to enhance the ministry of the church.

Post-Soul Test

1. Do you have any prejudices about hip hop?
2. If yes, what are they?
3. Do you believe hip hop can be positive, or is it only negative in your eyes?

4. Does your church have a ministry of the spoken word?
5. What is your greatest fear about implementing any of these principles?
6. Do you have youth and young adults running your technology ministry?
7. Have you surveyed your congregation to see who has artistic gifts?

Take these post-soul tests. Ask God to search your church's heart and reveal anything that might hinder your worship from pointing people to Christ in a way that resonates with their culture. Will we follow Christ even if he is walking among hip hoppers? It's time for more African American churches to develop a worship theology that is true to our roots, intentional about our mission, and relevant to the needs of our young people, the hip hop generation.

NOTES

1. Melville J. Herskovits, *The Myth of the Negro Past* (Boston: Beacon, 1958), 207–60.
2. James H. Evans Jr., *We Have Been Believers: An African-American Systematic Theology* (Minneapolis: Fortress, 1992), 11.
3. Carlyle Fielding Stewart, *African American Church Growth: Principles for Prophetic Ministry* (Nashville: Abingdon, 1994), 56.
4. Tricia Rose, *Black Noise: Rap Music and Black Culture in Contemporary America* (London: Wesleyan University Press, 1994).

BIBLIOGRAPHY

Baker, H. A., Jr. *Black Studies, Rap, and the Academy.* Chicago: University of Chicago Press, 1993.

Barna, G. *Evangelism That Works: How to Reach Changing Generations with the Unchanging Gospel.* Ventura, Calif.: Regal, 1995.

Best, C. *Culture @ the Cutting Edge: Tracking Caribbean Popular Music.* Jamaica: University Press of the West Indies, 2005.

Betha, P. M. *Revelations: There's a Light after the Lime.* New York: Atria, 2003.

Blount, B. K. *Cultural Interpretation: Reorienting New Testament Criticism.* Minneapolis: Fortress, 1995; reprint, Eugene, Ore.: Wipf & Stock, 2004.

Bogdanov, V. *All Music Guide to Hip-Hop: The Definitive Guide to Rap and Hip-Hop.* San Francisco: Backbeat Books, 2003.

Boyd, T. *Am I Black Enough for You? Popular Culture from the 'Hood and Beyond.* Bloomington: Indiana University Press, 1997.

———. *The New H.N.I.C. (Head Niggas in Charge): The Death of Civil Rights and the Reign of Hip Hop.* New York: New York University Press, 2004.

Braithwaite, F. *Fresh Fly Flavor: Words and Phrases of the Hip-Hop Generation.* Stamford, Conn.: Longmeadow, 1992.

BIBLIOGRAPHY

Brown, E. *Queens Reigns Supreme: Fat Cat, 50 Cent, and the Rise of the Hip Hop Hustler.* New York: Anchor, 2005.

Brown, J. *Jay-Z...And the Roc-a-fella Dynasty.* Phoenix: Amber Books, 2005.

Brown, S. *Tupac: A Thug Life.* London: Plexus, 2005.

Bynoe, Y. *Stand and Deliver: Political Activism, Leadership, and Hip Hop Culture.* Brooklyn, N.Y.: Soft Skull Press, 2004.

Cashin, S. *The Failures of Integration: How Race and Class Are Undermining the American Dream.* New York: PublicAffairs, 2004.

Cepeda, R. *And It Don't Stop: The Best American Hip-Hop Journalism of the Last 25 Years.* New York: Faber & Faber, 2004.

Chang, J., with introduction by DJ Kool Herc. *Can't Stop Won't Stop: A History of the Hip Hop Generation.* New York: St. Martin's, 2005.

Chideya, F. *Don't Believe the Hype: Fighting Cultural Misinformation about African Americans.* New York: Plume, 1995.

Chuck D, Yusuf Jah, and S. Lee. *Fight the Power: Rap, Race, and Reality.* New York: Delacorte, 1998.

Clark, K. B. *Dark Ghetto: Dilemmas of Social Power.* New York: Harper, 1965.

Cohn, N. *Triksta: Life and Death and New Orleans Rap.* New York: Knopf, 2005.

Coleman, B. *Rakim Told Me: Hip-Hop Wax Facts, Straight from the Original Artists, The 80s.* Somerville, Mass.: Wax Facts Press, 2005.

Coleman, W. *Tribal Talk: Black Theology, Hermeneutics, and African/American Ways of Telling the Story.* University Park: Pennsylvania State University Press, 2000.

Collins, P. H. *Black Sexual Politics: African Americans, Gender, and the New Racism.* New York: Routledge, 2004.

Curry, G. *The Best of Emerge Magazine.* New York: One World/Ballantine, 2003.

Cusic, D. *The Sound of Light: The History of Gospel and Christian Music.* Milwaukee: Hal Leonard Corporation, 2002.

Daniels, C. *Black Power Inc.: The New Voice of Success.* Hoboken, N.J.: John Wiley, 2004.

Darby, D., and T. Shelby, eds. *Hip Hop & Philosophy: Rhyme 2 Reason.* Chicago: Open Court, 2005.

Dee, K. M. *There's a God on the Mic: The True 50 Greatest MCs.* New York: Thunder's Mouth Press, 2003.

DMX, as told to S. D. Fontaine. *E.A.R.L.: Ever Always Real Life: The Autobiography of DMX.* New York: Harper Paperbacks, 2003.

Douglas, K. B. *The Black Christ.* Maryknoll, N.Y.: Orbis, 1994.

Dyson, M. E. *Between God and Gangsta Rap: Bearing Witness to Black Culture.* New York: Oxford University Press, 1997.

———. *Holler If You Hear Me: Searching for Tupac Shakur.* New York: Basic Civitas Books, 2002.

———. *Is Bill Cosby Right? Or Has the Black Middle Class Lost Its Mind?* New York: Basic Civitas Books, 2005.

———. *Mercy, Mercy Me: The Art, Loves, and Demons of Marvin Gaye.* New York: Basic Civitas Books, 2005.

Emery, A. *The Book of Hip Hop Cover Art.* London: Mitchell Beazley, 2004..

Fillingim, D. *Redneck Liberation: Country Music as Theology.* Macon, Ga.: Mercer University Press, 2003.

Forman, M. *The 'Hood Comes First: Race, Space, and Place in Rap and Hip-Hop.* Middletown, Conn.: Wesleyan University Press, 2002.

Frazier, E. F. *The Negro Church in America/The Black Church Since Frazier.* New York: Schocken, 1974.

Fresh, F. *The Rap Records 2004 Edition.* Minnesota: Nerby Publishing LLC, 2004.

Fricke, J. *Yes Yes Y'All: The Experience Music Project Oral History of Hip-Hop's First Decade.* Cambridge, Mass.: Da Capo, 2002.

Fynn, K. *Thugged Out.* Richmond, Calif.: Milligan Books, 2005.

Ganz, N. *Graffiti World: Street Art from Five Continents.* New York: Harry N. Abrams, 2004.

Gee, A., and J. Teter. *Jesus and the Hip-Hop Prophets: Spiritual Insights from Lauryn Hill and Tupac Shakur.* Downers Grove, Ill.: InterVarsity Press, 2003.

George, N. *The Death of Rhythm and Blues.* New York: Penguin, 1988.

———. *Hip Hop America.* New York: Penguin, 2005.

———. *Post-Soul Nation: The Explosive, Contradictory, Triumphant, and Tragic 1980s as Experienced by African Americans (Previously Known as Blacks and Before That Negroes).* New York: Viking Adult, 2004.

Gibbs, E. *ChurchNext: Quantum Changes in How We Do Ministry.* Downers Grove, Ill.: InterVarsity Press, 2000.

Gueraseva, S. *Def Jam, INC: Russell Simmons, Rick Ruben, and the Extraordinary Story of the World's Most Influential Hip-Hop Label.* New York: One World/Ballantine, 2005.

Guralnick, P. *Sweet Soul Music: Rhythm and Blues and the Southern Dream of Freedom.* New York: Back Bay Books, 1999.

Hilliard, D., Jr., with a foreword by H. H. Mitchell. *Church Growth from an African American Perspective.* Valley Forge, Pa.: Judson Press, 2006.

Hinds, S. S. *Gunshots in My Cook-Up: Bits and Bites from a Hip-Hop Caribbean Life.* New York: Atria, 2004.

hooks, b. *Salvation: Black People and Love.* New York: Harper Perennial, 2001.

———. *Where We Stand.* New York: Routledge, 2000.

hooks, b., and C. West. *Breaking Bread: Insurgent Black Intellectual Life.* Boston: South End Press, 1991.

Jenkins, S., et al. *Ego Trip's Book of Rap Lists.* New York: St. Martin's Griffin, 1999.

Jones, Q. *Tupac Shakur.* New York: Crown, 1998.

Kelley, R. D. G. *Race Rebels: Culture, Politics, and the Black Working Class.* New York: Free Press, 1996.

———. *Yo' Mama's Disfunktional! Fighting the Culture Wars in Urban America.* Boston: Beacon, 1998.

Keyes, C. L. *Rap Music and Street Consciousness.* Music in American Life. Urbana: University of Illinois Press, 2002.

Kitwana, B. *The Hip Hop Generation: Young Blacks and the Crisis in African American Culture.* New York: Basic Civitas Books, 2002.

———. *Why White Kids Love Hip Hop: Wangstas, Wiggers, Wannabes, and the New Reality of Race in America.* New York: Basic Civitas Books, 2005.

Krims, A. *Rap Music and the Poetics of Identity.* New Perspectives in Music History and Criticism. New York: Cambridge University Press, 2000.

Kukarui, N. *Hip Hop—Bring the Noise: The Stories Behind the Biggest Songs.* New York: Carlton Books, 2004.

Latifah, Q. *Ladies First: Revelations of a Strong Woman.* New York: William Morrow, 1999.

Light, A. *The Vibe History of Hip Hop.* New York: Three Rivers Press, 1999.

Lincoln, C. E., and L. H. Mamiya. *The Black Church in the African American Experience.* Durham, N.C.: Duke University Press, 1990.

Massey, D. S., and N. A. Denton. *American Apartheid: Segregation and the Making of the Underclass.* Cambridge, Mass.: Harvard University Press, 1993.

Mitchell, K. M. *Hip-Hop Rhyming Dictionary.* Los Angeles: Firebrand Music, 2003.

Miyakawa, F. M. *Five Percenter Rap: God Hop's Music, Message, and Black Muslim Mission.* Bloomington: Indiana University Press, 2005.

Morgan, J. *When Chickenheads Come Home to Roost: My Life as a Hip-Hop Feminist.* New York: Simon & Schuster, 1999.

Nuzum, E. D. *Parental Advisory: Music Censorship in America.* New York: Harper Collins, 2001.

Ogg, A., and D. Upshal. *The Hip Hop Years: A History of Rap.* New York: Fromm, 2001.

Oh, M., foreword by Ludacris. *Bling Bling: Hip Hop's Crown Jewels.* New York: Wenner, 2005.

Palmer, T. *Country Fried Soul: Adventures in Dirty South Hip-Hop.* San Francisco: Backbeat, 2005.

Parker, K. *Ruminations.* New York: Welcome Rain, 2003.

Pattillo-McCoy, M. *Black Picket Fences: Privilege and Peril among the Black Middle Class.* Chicago: University of Chicago Press, 2000.

Perkins, W. E. *Droppin' Science: Critical Essays on Rap Music and Hip Hop Culture.* Philadelphia: Temple University Press, 1995.

BIBLIOGRAPHY

Perry, I. *Prophets of the Hood: Politics and Poetics in Hip Hop.* Durham, N.C.: Duke University Press, 2004.

Pinn, A. B. *Noise and Spirit: The Religious and Spiritual Sensibilities of Rap Music.* New York: New York University Press, 2003.

———. *Varieties of African-American Religious Experience.* Minneapolis: Fortress, 1998.

Pough, G. D. *Check It While I Wreck It: Black Womanhood, Hip-Hop Culture, and the Public Sphere.* Boston: Northeastern University Press, 2004.

Powell, K. *Keepin' It Real: Post-MTV Reflections on Race, Sex, and Politics.* New York: One World/Ballantine, 1998.

———. *Who Shot Ya? Three Decades of Hip Hop Photography.* New York: Amistad, 2002.

Ptah, H. *A Hip-Hop Story.* New York: MTV Books, 2003.

Quinn, E. *Nuthin' but a "G" Thang: The Culture and Commerce of Gangsta Rap.* New York: Columbia University Press, 2004.

Ramsey, G. P., Jr. *Race Music: Black Cultures from Bebop to Hip-Hop.* Berkeley: University of California Press, 2003.

Rivera, R. Z. *New York Ricans from the Hip-Hop Zone.* New York: Palgrave Macmillan, 2003.

Ro, R. *Bad Boy: The Influence of Sean "Puffy" Combs on the Music Industry.* New York: Atria, 2001.

———. *Gangsta: Merchandising the Rhymes of Violence.* New York: St. Martin's, 1996.

———. *Raising Hell: The Reign, Ruin, and Redemption of Run-D.M.C. and Jam Master Jay.* New York: Amistad, 2005.

Rose, T. *Black Noise: Rap Music and Black Culture in Contemporary America.* London: Wesleyan University Press, 1994.

Run, R. *Words of Wisdom: Daily Affirmations of Faith.* New York: Amistad, 2006.

RZA, the, with C. Norris. *The Wu-Tang Manual.* New York: Riverhead Trade, 2005.

Shakur, T. A. *The Rose That Grew from Concrete.* New York: MTV Books/Pocket Books, 1999.

Shapiro, P. *The Rough Guide to Hip-hop.* 2nd rev. ed. London/New York: Rough Guides, 2005.

Smith, E., and P. Jackson. *The Hip-Hop Church: Connecting with the Movement Shaping Our Culture.* Downers Grove, Ill.: InterVarsity Press, 2006.

Smitherman, G. *Black Talk: Words and Phrases from the Hood to the Amen Corner.* New York: Houghton Mifflin, 2000.

Souljah, S. *No Disrespect.* New York: Vintage, 1996.

Spencer, J. M. *Blues and Evil.* Knoxville: University of Tennessee Press, 1993.

Steffans, K. *Confessions of a Video Vixen.* New York: Amistad, 2005.

Sylvan, R. *Traces of the Spirit: The Religious Dimensions of Popular Music*. New York: New York University Press, 2002.
Toop, D. *Rap Attack #3*. London: Serpent's Tail, 1999.

Wallace, V. *Biggie: Voletta Wallace Remembers Her Son, Christopher Wallace, aka Notorious B.I.G.* New York: Atria, 2005.

Wang, O. *Classic Material: The Hip-Hop Album Guide*. Toronto: ECW Press, 2003.

Watkins, S. C. *Hip Hop Matters: Politics, Pop Culture, and the Struggle for the Soul of a Movement*. Boston: Beacon, 2005.

———. *Representing: Hip Hop Culture and the Production of Black Cinema*. Chicago: University of Chicago Press, 1998.

Westbrook, A. *Hip Hoptionary TM: The Dictionary of Hip Hop Terminology*. New York: Harlem Moon, 2002.

White, A. *Rebel for the Hell of It: The Life of Tupac Shakur*. New York: Thunder's Mouth Press, 2002.

Williams, S. *The Dead Emcee Scrolls: The Lost Teachings of Hip-Hop and Connected Writings*. New York: MTV Books/Pocket Books, 2006.

Wilson, W. J. *The Ghetto Underclass: Social Science Perspectives*. Newbury Park, Calif.: Sage Publications, 1993.

———. *When Work Disappears: The World of the New Urban Poor*. New York: Alfred A. Knopf, 1996.

CPSIA information can be obtained
at www.ICGtesting.com
Printed in the USA
FSOW04n1048110617
34961FS

9 780817 015077